INFINITE MOBILIZATION

In memory of Jacob Taubes
1923–1987

Peter Sloterdijk

Infinite Mobilization

Towards a Critique of Political Kinetics

Translated by Sandra Berjan

polity

First published in German as *Eurotaoismus: Zur Kritik der politischen Kinetik*
© Suhrkamp Verlag, Frankfurt am Main, 1989

This English edition © Polity Press, 2020

Polity Press
65 Bridge Street
Cambridge CB2 1UR, UK

Polity Press
101 Station Landing
Suite 300
Medford, MA 02155, USA

ISBN-13: 978-1-5095-1847-0
ISBN-13: 978-1-5095-1848-7 (paperback)

A catalogue record for this book is available from the British Library.

Library of Congress Cataloging-in-Publication Data
Names: Sloterdijk, Peter, 1947- author. | Berjan, Sandra, translator.
Title: Infinite mobilization / Peter Sloterdijk ; translated by Sandra Berjan.
Other titles: Eurotaoismus. English
Description: English edition. | Cambridge, UK ; Medford, MA : Polity, 2020. | "First published in German as Eurotaoismus: Zur Kritik der politischen Kinetik, Suhrkamp Verlag Frankfurt am Main, 1989." | Includes bibliographical references and index. | Summary: "One of the world's leading philosophers shows how our preoccupation with motion and change is a defining feature of our modern, Western way of thinking"-- Provided by publisher.
Identifiers: LCCN 2019045590 (print) | LCCN 2019045591 (ebook) | ISBN 9781509518470 | ISBN 9781509518487 (paperback) | ISBN 9781509518517 (epub)
Subjects: LCSH: Political psychology--History--20th century. | Political sociology. | Europe--Politics and government--20th century. | Europe--Civilization--History.
Classification: LCC JA74.5 .S5813 2020 (print) | LCC JA74.5 (ebook) | DDC 320.01--dc23
LC record available at https://lccn.loc.gov/2019045590
LC ebook record available at https://lccn.loc.gov/2019

Typeset in 10.5 on 12pt Times
by Fakenham Prepress Solutions, Fakenham, Norfolk, NR21 8NL
Printed and bound in Great Britain by TJ International Limited

The publisher has used its best endeavours to ensure that the URLs for external websites referred to in this book are correct and active at the time of going to press. However, the publisher has no responsibility for the websites and can make no guarantee that a site will remain live or that the content is or will remain appropriate.

Every effort has been made to trace all copyright holders, but if any have been overlooked the publisher will be pleased to include any necessary credits in any subsequent reprint or edition.

For further information on Polity, visit our website:
politybooks.com

Contents

Premises

The original German title of this book used the cumbersome and speculative word "Eurotaoism."[1] Why was this necessary?

There are three possible answers to this question. First, this could be an instance of those involuntary and nonsensical turns of phrase that I have been shown to let slip rather frequently; if this is true, we might as well assume that the book has already died of its own title as though from an overdose of profundity. Second, what we could have here is an example of combinatorial wit in the style of Friedrich Schlegel's shotgun weddings of two vastly differing terms; but should such wit truly be in play, we had better leave it unexplained – wit that supplies its own discussion is no longer witty. However, since combinatorics is a tried and true early romanticist method for the discovery of structural analogues, a request for patience may be permitted in order to await the result. Third, "Eurotaoism" could be the heading above a missed opportunity. Such a title lends itself so easily to saying something groundbreaking about the play of polarities, the reunification of spirit and nature, and the opening of the heart chakra. All these things are of concern to us. I admit that it is a shame when an opportunity is missed to assure readers that they, too, have the divine within them. But denying the facts leads nowhere; there is nothing uplifting in what follows. This book and its title linger solely in problematic terrains – its appeal is exclusively aimed at the need to understand what drives the current course of the world in the direction it is going. Addressing the needs of intelligence in this way is still valid, even if we have to admit that the proposed exercises in comprehension seem like the gesticulations of a streetlamp lighter who wants to make himself useful in a city that has switched to neon lighting.

These answers will no doubt disappoint. Clearly, this is not so much about precise inquiries as an evasive maneuver in the face of embarrassment. But was an affirmative answer really to be expected? The Tao in the mouths of Western writers ... is it not just a Joker card one plays when it comes to promising more than can be delivered? Oh, Taoism! Magic formula for immediate wholeness and lab-made safety, courtesy of atomic physics! The enigmatic syllable "Tao" has recently fallen into the category of kitsch, and those who henceforth commit themselves to its bright magic will be suspected of having joined the New Age choir singing holistic couplets. But I consider it *a priori* the very center of my work to make myself available for suspicion. After all, philosophers have previously only questioned the interpretation of the world made by other people – it is necessary to engage in it.

"Eurotaoism" – to hint at a more serious answer – is also a title for the attempt to call attention to the peculiarity of the history-making continent in such an urgent way that a merely superficial critique of it can no longer become plausible. Even if we recognize Eastern wisdom as an impressive and singular greatness, Asian imports alone will not save the Western-mobilized world. The initiative of "Americotaoism" is just that – a response to the "crisis of the West" by importing holistic fast food from the Far East. Of course, this fast food sells itself as Nouvelle Cuisine; it relies on innovation as if it were an irresistible recipe, serves up planetary paradigm shifts like courses on a traditional menu, and earnestly promises that the raw fish course will be followed by a tender Aquarian chop-suey. But as one might fear, the scope of New Thinking amounts to nothing more than suggesting that we eat our ideas with chopsticks from now on – "you are what you eat."

The present response concedes the validity of such Californian suggestions where they have their place. It serves to remind, however, as humbly as possible and as defiantly as necessary, that there are dishes – to stay with the metaphor – that would leave us hungry with chopsticks in our hand. And these are – literally speaking now – the large-scale phenomena which emerged from the Old European epistemic-messianic substance and became effective on a planetary scale: history, science, industry, mass communication, speed. Even if these are not a constant topic of discussion, the essays in this field constantly gravitate around them. They form the criteria for thought capable of thinking the present. In the face of such thorny phenomena, it may seem like mockery to quote the round world of ancient Chinese polarities. If the title of this book nevertheless does so, it is to recall the ironic scope of self-generated problems at the place where the launching pads of the modernizing expeditions were mounted. From there on out, one would have to be a Taoist to endure the insight that even Taoism can't help us anymore.

Why, then, Eurotaoism? In this strange word we hear the remaining echoes of the history-making discontent that drove the great revolutions of modernity. We also hear it chime astonishment that nothing better came out of the European uprisings into the new than the all too current drift towards catastrophe. As a picaresque term, it has something of that "jaded bitterness" from which the guiding intellectual forces of earlier times wanted to distill the knowledge of revolution. But wearing a jester's hat, the word now heralds an alternative critique of modernity – a critique of planetary mobilization as a false permanent revolution. Coupled with the subtitle – "Towards a Critique of Political Kinetics" – the term gradually becomes reasonable in a rather crazy way. This is also evident by the fact that it will no longer play a role in what is to follow. The word appears only once more – the reader will have to guess to what purpose.

Like all that I have previously published, these texts are subversive exercises against the absolutism of history and socialization. Instead of orienting ourselves by the progressive norm that so quickly degenerates to a forward crawl, I recommend being attentive to sideways mobility. That is what the recourse to the ancient cynical intervention and the allusion to the utopian sharp wit of the man in the barrel were about, only in a more indirect and ambiguous way. In the meantime, the amusement over the critique of cynicism has dissipated; among those capable of judgment, nothing remains of the misunderstanding that critique would thus be reduced to mere pantomime. The thing that always emerges from the discovery of pantomime – the understanding of gesture, gesticulation, and movement – has crossed over into suggestions for a theory of civilizing movement; a theory in which the life-or-death difference between mobility and mobilization presents itself as criterion of an alternative "ethics." Thus, the following pages contain a new version of critical theory in its embryonic form – not of "society" but of the Western type of progressive process that is played out by modern societies. In the current world process, which exhibits an accelerated movement towards catastrophe, people – as the perpetrators and victims of mobilization – experience their predominant life form as something that leads the wrong way. In their characteristics as perpetrators, they at the same time learn of their ability to be so completely in agreement with the trend towards the wrong thing that they identify with it. Thus, a critical theory of mobilization is not just a translation of the critique of alienation into a language of kinetics. One has to assume that within the most hazardous accelerations of the present, something is executed that stems from what is our own, what is closest to us – in other words, something self-intended. If this is the case, then a critical theory of society is no longer possible, since there is no actual difference between the critique itself and the object of that critique – unless the critique would first turn its thinking against itself and then also examine what is of one's own, nearest and self-intended, as well.

This kind of critique has so far only existed in the form of theology. Theologians have enjoyed the prerogative to critique the world as such in the name of an Other that is superior to the world, so that that which is one's own was also subject to criticism. In this book, I attempt to repeat a critique of this kind in a non-theological way. This presupposes that the critical spirit can break away from the world to distance and transform what is one's own, nearest and self-intended, too. Such a critique explodes the cynical-melancholy notion of a fallen world, one that nowadays sells itself everywhere as post-modern acceptance. It also eschews masochistic total contemplation, which leads to a metaphysical "drop-out-ism." Neither escapist nor in agreement, the goal of alternative critique is to advance a critical theory of being-in-the-world. It would become plausible in the moment it successfully indicated a non-theological space for distance from the world – opened up a transcendence for the purpose of methodology, if you will. I am of the opinion that we are at the beginning stages of such a theory. Its center forms an analytics of coming-into-the-world[2] where the position of philosophical anthropology that humans are "here" loses its validity – we may no longer carelessly assume that "existence" and "being-in-the-world" can be attributed to humans. The presumption that "human beings" are already "in the world" and "exist" becomes corrected by a Socratic maieutic method that deals with arriving on earth and generating worlds, as well as the risk of failure associated with both efforts. What was previously considered to be existential philosophy becomes transformed into a cosmology of the individual – each birth is a chance for a world to sprout up. Maieutic philosophy speaks of the exertion that actually emerging individuals must generate in order to *be there*. What is thus brought into discussion follows the movement of the life that comes into the world. In this way, the maieutic method once again speaks a serious language – a dramatic world language about the commonly inevitable.

As we will see, only trace elements of these kinds of reflections have previously been available to us in an explicit way – elements that inhabit the space between Heidegger and Bloch, Cioran and

Lao Tzu (a space that is barely still surveyed or even perceived). Nevertheless it must be said – to avoid creating confusion – that the explicit elements of the following will appear obscure without the implicit. The reflections steer towards the thesis that the idea of critique without reserves against the unreasonable demands of the world will remain hollow. The question of whether a critical theory is still possible depends on resolving the problem of whether an enlightened a-cosmism may not be a necessary mode of lucid life.[3]

It is no wonder that serious tones predominate in this book. Other tones have joined the amoral cabaret that wanted to save itself from tragedy. The Teutonic vein in particular stands out more noticeably, weighing down the carefree cheer of the otherwise preferred Southern tone. Thin vibrations of Chinese elements add themselves to the mix and a fatal music of the spheres is barely perceptible against the death march of hardness, strength, skill. It would also be wrong to deny that, here and there, a Jewish cantor's world lament can be heard, for whom every man-made wall becomes a Wailing one. The dedication to Jacob Taubes – one of the last great representatives of the Jewish spirit in the German language – who died in March 1987, holds a commitment to the memory of apocalypticism as a Jewish alternative to the optimism of the moderns and the tragicism of neo-heroics. It is in Taubes' work that I experienced an unforgettable enlightenment about that which Manés Sperber calls the religion of good memory.

A nuance will surely elude a reader who is unfamiliar with the landscape where these texts largely came into being. In them, at least to my perception, some of that ahistorical calm of a Provençal summer has been stored. They assume a refutation of city neuroses through heat and light; you may sense the spirit of that place in the way that thoughts at the end of a given paragraph do not always continue on logically – there are frequent imperceptible interruptions between one sentence and the next. The warmth of the land seeps into these gaps – a land that rests upon itself in a burning euphoria. In such a climate, one's very physiological functions change. Thinking automatically becomes a measure against the heat even though it cannot entirely help but become a symptom of it as well – cruelly rested, it glints at the reader mischievously, as if offering an invitation to a long siesta; it seems to be joviality itself at play. Sitting at Northern desks, one might not be able to immediately pick up on these conditions because different requirements apply to them. Nevertheless, to understand the matters at hand, one must go to the countryside from time to time. The task of discovering a slower pace applies to philosophy as well.

The more horses you hitch up, the faster it goes – I mean, not tearing the block out of the foundations, which is impossible, but tearing the reins and so travelling empty and joyful.

Franz Kafka[4]

1

THE MODERN AGE AS MOBILIZATION

May your fate be to live in interesting times.
Ancient Chinese curse

Can humans still comprehend the general development of the modern world that they have set in motion? A growing list of contemporaries denies that it is possible – their answers are based on arguments and not just instinctual reactions. For this reason, there is much talk of a post-modern condition at the end of this interesting century.[1] But the inscrutable aspects of our times are so uniquely new that we must not equate our current confusions of the mind with pre-modern surrenders of human reason when confronted with the mysteries of the world.

One idea has rooted itself in pre-modern ways of thinking more deeply than any other: nothing turns out the way it was planned. For even though man may propose, it is still the gods who dispose, whatever the case may be. The *a priori* of any Old World practical life experience is: if it happens as it should, it happens differently than it was planned. This experience cannot rid itself of the constant awareness that human plans and actions always move in the recesses of an insurmountable passivity. But with the advent of modernity, things happen in a new way – just as humans have planned. They do so because people in the West, monks, merchants, physicians, architects, painters, and cannon-makers – *in summa* geniuses and engineers – have begun to organize their way of thinking in an entirely new way; and (one would like to say, suddenly) a new kind of "praxis" joins this reorganization of thought as the technological counterpart of thinking and intervenes in the events of the world with a revolutionary impact. Modernity as a techno-political composite has unhinged the old familiar equilibrium between human power and powerlessness. Spurred on by a history-making amalgam of aggression and optimism, modernity promises us a world in which things turn out as planned because people are able to accomplish what they want – and if not, they are able and willing to learn. In modern times, it is the will to power of the can-do spirit that makes the world go around.

It is for one reason only that we call our epoch modern: people of the West have been so captivated and impressed by their own great deeds that they found the courage to proclaim that they had created the world on their own. This and nothing else constitutes the very core of what we (often defensively) refer to as the project of modernity. This project nature of the modern era stems from the grand assumption that we will soon be able to control the world to such an extent that nothing continues to develop unless we wisely choose to maintain it with our own actions. The modern project is thus established on the basis of a *kinetic utopia* – something that has never been explicitly articulated: the total movement of the world is to be the implementation of our plans for it. The movements of our day-to-day lives become progressively identical with the movement of the world itself; the process of the world as a whole increasingly resembles an expression of our lives – things occur as planned because that which occurs is increasingly an event of our making. It would not suffice to say that modernity set out to make history from this point forward. At its innermost core, modernity wants to create nature in addition to history. As this evil century draws to a close, it dawns on us that making history was just a pretext. The crucial issue of the modern era is the nature that is to be made.

As soon as modernity's kinetic utopia is revealed, its seemingly stable foundation cracks open and new problems come to light – what we have learned in the good old modern age no longer applies to anything. The paradoxes displayed by the very developments of the modern era constitute the thus newly formed and unusual problem world: a post-history superimposes itself onto history, an epinature onto nature, and a post-modernity onto modernity. Meanwhile, the inevitable transformation of modernity into post-modernity becomes obvious to any onlooker. It results from the observation that even modern events occur differently than planned – but not because man proposes and god disposes; rather, this notion that "it must occur differently" is both inherent in and not quite understood by our thoughts and actions, and it pushes right through our venture with an unstoppable irony. Things do not happen according to plan because we have left movement out of the calculation. Things unfailingly do not happen according to plan because as we think through and bring forth what is supposed to occur, we automatically set in motion something else as a by-product – something we did not think about, did not want, and failed to consider. Once set in motion, it propels itself forward with a dangerous tenacity. It seems that we have surrounded ourselves with an epinature of consequences that slip away from the grasp of our "history-making" praxis like a secondary physis. With mounting unease, we watch as the self-perpetuating side-effects of modern progress spill over into the controlled projects; a fatally foreign movement breaks off from this very core of the modern enterprise, from within the consciousness of a spontaneous independence that is guided by reason – and it slips away from us in every direction. What looked like a controlled uprising towards freedom turns out to be a slide into an uncontrollable and catastrophic hetero-mobility. Precisely because so much comes about *through* our actions, just as we have planned, developments as a whole turn out explosively and affect us quite differently.

This is the post-modern *status quo*, and it is actually a *lapsus* – a regressive step. A philosophical post-modernism made up of insights and not merely nostalgic posturing or bad moods can only be possible today because, given the actual course of events, powerful arguments make it clear that the bubble of modernity's kinetic utopia has burst. Unforeseen processes have gained momentum, and it is doubtful whether humans can ever rein them back in and divert them to a trajectory that will not prove fatal.

If we were to give a philosophical name to the drift of the current "civilizing process" (a dreadful term that burns the tongue), we would have to say that it resembles a thinking avalanche. What is a thinking avalanche? We do not know, but it is certainly what we are. We were hardly predictable as such, but this astounding avalanche is nevertheless plunging towards the valley as we speak. The "civilizing process" (the tongue begins to ache) turns out to be a pressing ontological oddity. What becomes a given in this process is nothing other than a self-reflexive natural catastrophe. And like all that is calamitous, this, too, is philosophically very interesting. The thinking avalanche is the industrial post-Christian counterpart to Pascal's thinking reed, which once upon a time trembled in the icy breath of the early modern era. Meanwhile, the most fragile of all creatures, the human, avalanche *qui pense*, is no longer endangered by the storm of life alone – he is himself setting off the landslides that can bury him alive.

Leaving these rather lyrical intimations behind, we will now turn to the analytical and feel our way forward through the no-man's-land between old concepts and new circumstances. Now more than ever, a critique of the current times must begin with the admission that we do not know how things happen to us. We will begin by seeking that which is incomprehensible, unwritten, and overlooked in the current "civilizing process." At this point, it might only be possible to establish a few bridgeheads of articulation in the blind and murky vortex of events. I do not go so far as to claim that an alternative "critical theory" of the modern age could already take shape in these pages. What I do claim is merely this: first, that both of the well-known versions of critical theory (the Marxist and Frankfurt Schools primarily come to mind) have up to now remained irrelevant because either they do not grasp their object – the kinetic reality of modernity as mobilization – or they are unable to point out a critical difference to it because they are mobilizers themselves based on the effect they have; second, that diagnoses of present times must be brought into a kinetic and kinesthetic dimension because if they are not, all talk of modernity bypasses what is most real. The following diagnostic exercises are post-modern only insofar as they stem from a readiness to formulate the modern active voice into the passive voice. To think from a post-modern position is to explicitly own up to the congestion, vortices, vacuities, and depressions that come with the kind of spontaneity that the modern era has triggered. With respect to philosophy, the post-modern can perhaps best be recognized by its reformulation of modernity's strong and proud sentences in the active voice into those in either passive or impersonal phrases. What is thereby revealed is not only a grammatical engagement but also an ontological one – what is at stake is nothing less than the possibility to include suffering, incidents, and processes in our contemporary idea of "being" alongside deeds, dates, and productions. Modernity has overfed us with theories of action – what it knew of suffering is only that it could be "used" as an engine for actions. But what if the necessity to develop a passionate consciousness of human mortality arose from today's numerous cultural approaches to post-modernism; a consciousness of a second passivity that can only develop on the flipside of the project that is modernity? Seen from the point of view of a second passivity, what does the historically moved world mean? What meaning does the made and to-be-made history retain for us, of which leading modern philosophers have expected so much? If the modern era really was a revolt of the subject against its first passivity – some say it was a campaign to disrupt fate – what is to be made, then, of the second passivity that weighs on history as suffering, on our ability to make history as anxiety, and on this dubious enterprise called modern life as a compulsion to participate in it?

At the margins of modernity, history and fate engage yet again in unforeseen duels. It is as if a quasi-karmic debit interrupts the deeds and doers in history to undermine their very projects and intentions. We will investigate this "karmic" irony in kinetic terms. For it is clear that neither the philosophy of history proper nor classical Eastern concepts of karma (i.e. moral causality of actions) can adequately interpret the fact that things occur differently than planned in modern times. Thus, it is neither the fault of the antagonist in the most recent battle[2] nor due to an unpaid karmic debt of the actors that a history planned with the best intentions does not succeed. The historical movement gets out of hand because of the inherent aspects of making history. Whoever moves always moves more than just themselves. Whoever makes history always makes more than just history. This "more" is the typo that distorts the neatly drawn-up text – it is the kinetic surplus which shoots beyond borders and past targets into a region not aimed for. The fatal "more" joins the momentum of the dead masses who have forgotten all about moral purposes once in motion. This kinetic capital blows up old worlds – it has nothing against them; it simply cannot be stopped on principle. It cannot help but make affairs dance to accelerated melodies. It makes the flow of goods flow, fleets cruise, escalators glide, climates suddenly change, and faunas disappear. The naïve times in which humans could think that their movement was necessary for the world to move forward are over. Meanwhile, the movement goes on – the pure movement. While the gracious defenders of modern accomplishments bow down to theories of human actions and talk about the norms of the (latest) reasons for acting (they will certainly be promoted to directors of the future national parks of modernity), an ugly suspicion makes its rounds in the rest of the world: could kinetics and fate be one and the same?

The Mobilization of the Planet from the Spirit of Self-Intensification

The following interpretation of the present is based on philosophical kinetics, which assumes three axioms: first, that we move in a world that is itself in motion; second, that the self-movement of the world both includes and surpasses our self-movement; third, that in modernity, the self-movements of the world emerge out of our self-movements, which are cumulatively added to world-movement. From these axioms, we can more or less completely develop the relationship between the Old World, the modern world, and the post-modern world.

To show the modern world as one engaged in a catastrophe-bearing movement, we would have to assume that today's world process received its dynamism from centuries of accumulated human initiatives. Thus, perceiving the modern age with an awareness of real events means accepting something that our intellectual conscience has resisted so far: a physics of freedom, a kinetics of moral initiatives. Let us say it openly: this is the end of aestheticism in cultural theory. What seems emptiest, most external, most mechanical – movement (ungrudgingly left to the physicists and doctors of sports medicine to research) – intrudes into the humanities and immediately proves to be the cardinal category of the moral and social spheres as well.

Marked by movement, the ethical-political adventures of the human mind become a branch of physics. While everywhere in the West ethics commissions hold meetings, while people of good will sacrifice their weekends in order to discuss the principles of a New Morality in idyllically located evangelical academies and political "study centers," modernity's best-kept secret seeps out of the studios of hermetic and philosophical fundamental research into the open. What nobody really wanted to know becomes increasingly evident. What nobody welcomed as an insight forces itself into our thoughts with a logical rigor that is altogether infuriating. Once spoken aloud, the revealed secret makes us wonder why something so obvious has not been brought to our attention long ago. Some urbanists and a few military people who liked to speculate knew it first; dodgy philosophers who mistrusted modernity adopted the matter; the wild eccentrics in the theory scenes of big cities jumped on the bandwagon; a few mundane feature articles in the culture and arts pages of newspapers and magazines took up the issue; soon many will claim that they have always known it. Known what, then? Well, the trivial fact that kinetics is the ethics of modernity.

The worrisome and even obscene nature of this emerging fact is only partially alleviated by relating it to well-known doctrines of progress. There, the liaison between kinetics and morality still seemed to be controlled morally. Indeed, modernity has also been defined in kinetic terms since the beginning, having had its manner of execution and realization determined to be progressive and forward-thinking. Progress is the concept of movement in which the ethical-kinetic self-awareness of modernity is both expressed and concealed to the highest degree. If we are talking about progress, what we really mean is the kinetic and kinesthetic ground motive of a modernity that only aims to remove the limits of human self-movement. Initially we assumed (both rightly and wrongly) that progress is a "moral" initiative which would not rest until it actualized its goals of improvement. The experience of a true progress entails that a worthwhile human initiative stems "from within itself," burst the bounds of its previous mobility, widen its circle of influence, and bring itself to the fore in good conscience vis-à-vis both its inner inhibitions and outside resistance.

The current epoch has expressed its kinetic self-conception in doctrines of progress in the fields of politics, technology, and the philosophy of history. But it never revealed its secret tendency to take moral motives seriously only in their capacity as motors for external movement. Part of the essence of progressive processes is that they begin with ethical initiatives so that they can continue in their kinetic momentum alone. One of the great secrets of "progress" still remains: how could it at its onset fuse mores and physics, motives and movement into an effective unit? This secret leads us to the active center of what modern philosophy calls subjectivity. The essence of subjectivity is inseparable from the mysterious force that expresses itself as the ability to initiate *new* chains of movement which we label "actions." If something like progress really exists, then it does so because movements that originate in subjectivity undeniably occur. Kinetically, these are the very material from which modernity is built. Whenever the thought of "progress" goes through the mind of a subject, the self-igniting mechanism within that thought already initiates progress-like self-movements. The person who truly knows what progress is already moves within what has been conceptualized – they know it, because they have already progressed and continue to progress further. The person who grasps modernity can only grasp it on the basis of this self-igniting self-movement, without which modernity would not exist. Already in their self-creation, they must have taken a good step forward – the very step that continues to be the very kinetic element of further progress. Progress is initiated by this step into a second step, one that performs its own self-introduction in order to then surpass itself. This is why the notion of progress does not signify a mere change of location where an agent moves from point A to point B. A "step" is essentially only progressive if it leads to an increase in the "ability to take steps." This provides us with the formula of the modernizing process: progress is movement towards movement, movement towards greater movement, and movement towards an increased ability to move.

In modernity, ethics can directly emerge from kinetics only due to the validity of this formula. Ethical imperatives of the modern kind no longer exist, unless they are also simultaneously kinetic impulses. The categorical impulse of modernity is: in order to continuously exert ourselves as progressive beings, we should overcome all situations in which humans are constricted in their movements, stuck within themselves, without freedom and pitiful.[3]

To the extent that we as modern subjects understand freedom to be *a priori* the freedom of movement, we can only conceive of progress as a movement that leads to increased mobility. In their physical sense, free movements are always steps towards freedom of movement; even when we speak of self-determination, we really always mean self-movement. Prior to any difference between "is" and "ought," "being" is determined in modernity as an "ought to be" and an "I want to be" of increased mobility. Ontologically, modernity is a pure being-towards-movement. This interpretation of "being" is valid *for us* because it becomes irresistibly real *through us*. It is irresistibly valid because it is immune to backlash and morally ruinous for any negation of it. It becomes real because it is carried out by us in the mode of a spontaneous and uncriticizable will. The motives that pulsate in the being-towards-movement seem to come from the inner core of what we want and have to want. If the fundamental process of modernity indeed advertises itself as the "self-freeing movement of humankind," then it is a process that we do not utterly wish to reject and a movement that we absolutely cannot make. A moral-kinetic automatism seems to be at work here – one that makes us not only "condemned to be free"[4] but also to be in constant free movement.

If we visualize the great revolutions of the modern world as occurring on the scale of our own lives, we notice a profound contradiction in our steps towards a higher degree of movement. To be sure, the thrusts towards movement of modern generations have provided us with enormous leeway in numerous fields – what members of the modern bourgeoisie have been able to attain within the span of hardly two centuries with respect to mobility in the field of politics, economy, language, information, traffic, expression, and sexuality borders on the miraculous; herein a kinetic "modern tradition" becomes evident, regardless of how questionable the possibility of its continuation may be. But instead of guiding the agents of modernity to spirited[5] mobility, most of the steps of progress have immediately led to new kinds of forced movements which compete with the most stifling endings of pre-modern times in their depth of alienation and misery.

Modern "dynamism" helped preserve the spiritless rigor of super-mobile forms. Whoever wishes to know what this specifically means must answer the following question correctly: what do machines, industrial companies, and management staff in politics and economics have in common? All three hold the exemplary kinetic lesson for citizens of modernity by efficiently demonstrating to them what self-movement wants and does: to switch itself on in order to stay on; to activate itself in order to stay running at any cost. This is the higher school of automation which sees no fundamental difference between intelligent machines and human agents. If the kinetic self activates and takes the initiative, it turns into the central agency of the self-operating process via its "own" impetus.

The self-initiating subject is the miller of modernity's "mill grinding itself" – this is what the poet Novalis in his 1799 essay "Christendom or Europe" called the principle of movement of the then activated human-nature factory that gained momentum through prosaic self-motivating entrepreneurial types: Protestants, Brits, Prussians, and professors. Novalis was also the first to conceptualize the kinetic utopia of modernity by thinking the subject and the machine together in the same image: the "mill of itself" is the "true *perpetuum mobile*" that is "driven by the stream of chance and floating on it,"[6] uniting two kinds of movement (endogenous self-movement and exogenous foreign movement) into a consolidated motion – a motion whose dynamism is admittedly also its bleakness – an ego-driven drift into vacuity, catastrophe, lack of inhibition, and deadliness.

The diagnostic power of Novalis' formulations is only today becoming apparent to us in its full scope. Meanwhile, we now know (without the help of even a hint of romantic irony) *what* the self manages to do in "its" machine, even if this machine is not exactly a self-grinding mill. Modern society has realized at least one of its utopian plans, namely that of total automobilization – the state in which every self that is of age moves on its own at the wheel of its self-moving machine. It is because the modern self cannot be thought of at all without the notion of *its* movement that the I and the automobile belong together in a metaphysical way, like the body and soul of one and the same unit of motion. The automobile is the technological double of the principally active transcendental subject.

That is why the automobile is the sanctum of modernity; it is the cultish center of a kinetic world religion; it is the sacrament on wheels that lets us take part in something that moves faster than we do. A person who drives a car gets closer to the numinous and feels how their small self expands to a higher self that makes the total world of highways into a home for us and makes us aware that we are called to something more than a half-animal pedestrian life.

From an auto-motorist view, we lived in Messianic time for a little while, in the fulfilled time where two-cycle engine vehicles parked peacefully next to twelve-cylinder vehicles – the messiah ruled with low emissions in his kingdom; with electronic fuel injection and an anti-locking system, with a controlled catalyst and turbo charger, he brought his subjects into heavenly motion. But not all contemporaries were convinced that this last kingdom of automobiles was also a paradise on earth. The devil had a part to play and made sure to occasionally turn general self-movement into general immobility. In such moments it becomes clear – even if no one wants to admit it to themselves – that we have long been exiled from the paradise of modernity and will have to learn the post-modern Stop-and-Go by the sweat of our brow from now on. The large-scale traffic jams on the summer highways of Central Europe (and the legendary power outages in New York that can make us feel nostalgic) are thus phenomena of historico-philosophical importance and even have a religio-historical significance. It is through them that a piece of false modernity fails and in them that we encounter the end of an illusion – they are the kinetic Good Friday when all hope for redemption through acceleration becomes lost. On those scorching afternoons in the funnel of Lyon, in the Rhine valley hell near Cologne, or wedged in at Irschenberg, Europe's longest parking lot, where 1.5 miles of unmoving hot steel stretches out in either direction, dark historico-philosophical insights rise up like exhaust fumes and people begin to speak in tongues, uttering something critical about contemporary culture; obituaries of modernity waft from the side windows and, regardless of their educational level, those trapped in their vehicles begin to suspect that it cannot go on like this for much longer. Another "era" looms on the horizon. Even those who have never heard the term "post-modernity" are already familiar with what it entails on those afternoons spent in traffic. And in fact, this can be reformulated in terms of cultural theory: wherever unleashed self-movements form congestions or vortices, they generate the beginnings of an experience where the modern active turns into the post-modern passive.

What can we gain from these flickering observations that could lead to a serious theory of the present? They accomplish enough for what is to follow if they help build up suggestions that generate the next step forward. That step is to openly appoint the term "mobilization" as the core expression to explain and describe the basic process of modernity. Without hasty consideration of the inevitable horror at such a choice of concept and its inherent consequences, it is first a matter of strengthening the evidence that modernizations always show the character of mobilizations in a kinetic way. Of course, one could proceed inductively and discreetly with so-called "infantry" methods, collecting countless peripheral descriptions of the current *status-lapsus-quo* of the processes in the bio- and noosphere in a slow accumulation of evidence: the number of revenue billionaires is multiplying; the butterflies of our childhoods are no longer there; the trajectories of long-distance tourism and arms budgets are showing a significant upward trend; the populations in modernizing countries are exploding while those in already modernized countries are stagnant; the holes in the ozone layer above the poles are aggressively widening; sneaker sales are flourishing while those of surf gear are sinking; trees in low mountain ranges are becoming discolored and forming brush-like crowns; South African fruit can presently be found at Bavarian Sunday markets; the air time of Soviet nuclear bullets is 120 seconds from the Urals to Bad Godesberg, and so on. But the endless number of such statements only makes sense if they find a common denominator in the term "mobilization," which makes an essential assertion about several separate processes: the essence of what is happening today are proceedings of mobilization. The very diversity of varied interpretations of modernity is what forms it according to a kinetic model since that model can be identified as that of a mobilization.

It is very right to take offense at the military connotations of the term at first. Mobilization is a category belonging to a world of wars – it encompasses the critical processes by which dormant combat potentials are brought to readiness for action. The aversion towards the concept referred to by the term, and even more so the disgust towards the actual procedure, must not make us blind to the fact that the kinetic foundational model of this process – as self-actualization for deployment – is by no means specific only to the military but rather expresses the foundational principle of modern self-moving enterprises as a whole. The aesthetic shudder as a response to the word could easily seduce us to abandon the only term that makes the dynamic model of modernization nameable. We are unable to avoid thinking of certain notorious works by Ernst Jünger in this context, who famously already in the early 1930s dislodged the phenomenon of mobilization from its military-specific meaning in order to apply it to the process of modern society as a whole. For half a century now these statements have been lying on the trash heap of intellectual history – unused, scandal-ridden, unacceptable, but above all untested, hated rather than refuted, unchosen rather than outdated. There is a reason for the general reservations against Jünger's reflections, which have been suspected of being fascist. Whoever would adopt his cold, evil optic for an analysis of late modern processes even on a trial basis risks experiencing a historico-philosophical Damascus. Far beyond Jünger's intentions, the category of mobilization can liberate insights that are not compatible with the sleep of the just in the project of modernity. The ominous formula of "total mobilization" prepares the still scandalous and, yes, even almost unbearable realization that a political-kinetic fundamental process exists in the modern world whose tendency is to *de facto* neutralize the morally important difference between work and war and increasingly override the once existing distinction between rest position and deployment. This is precisely the uncanny process of mobilization – to bring everything considered a power reserve to the "front" and drive any potential forward towards realization. Jünger is that evil man whom we will always quote from a great distance – though of course never without respect for his perceptual capacity;[7] but his exercises generated a previously unobtained definition of modern technology as the "mobilization of the planet via the figure of the worker." Of course, the latter does not describe the Marxist subject of history, the proletariat, but rather the planetary subject of mobilization, trembling from over-fitness, the pain-hardened, matter-of-fact high-performance type in his dedicated effort to the self-exalting, readying, forward- and perhaps future-looking action system (whether we call it a company, class, people, nation, bloc, or country is already irrelevant on this level of action).

If we now want to undertake a new attempt under very different constellations to make the term "mobilization" productive for a new theory of modernity (of course, very differently from Jünger, the order of merit wearer), it will only be promising insofar as we accept the discomfort with the term and place it in the service of a critical perspective. This term will keep alive the memory of the violent core of the major scientific, military, and industrial processes, especially at a time when they are entering a smart phase where violence is becoming informational, cool, procedural, and analgesic. (What is the key phrase of the new phase again? Transfer from heavy industry to fast information? Transition from working society to learning society? The first would probably give off a little soot, the second will be as clean as the toilets in a Swiss motorway rest stop.) Precisely because the term "mobilization" (owing to the uncanny, even disastrous elements in its meaning) bristles against a total positivism (Jünger's nerves-of-steel attempt in this direction cannot be repeated), it is more appropriate than any other to describe a "civilizing" mechanism that exploits all modern growth of skill, knowledge, mobility, precision, and effectiveness for processes of crowding out and killing off, for upgrades, expansions, self-authorization, and breaches of context. Mobilization as an autogenous fundamental process of modernity leads to the provision of ever-increasing movement potentials for position holding, which precisely by way of the conditions and effects of this deployment make themselves impossible as positions and drift into the untenable. It is here that the broad field of kinetic paradoxes opens up for an alternate critique of modernity. Thus, social critique becomes a critique of false mobility.

If, after the debacle of Marxism and the ambiguous fading away of the Frankfurt Schools, there can still be a third version of critical theory of a sophisticated kind, then it is probably only in the form of a critical theory of movement. If it is to be accurate, its therapeutic criteria would consist of the difference between correct movement and false mobilization. Its claim to truth would rest on the recognition that a kinetic spectrum exists that reaches from physiology all the way to politics. A critical theory of mobilization would bridge the gap between the thought process and the actual event on the level of basic terms – there would no longer be any "outside" thinking; the theorist would have to ask herself at every sentence whether what she is doing increases the offering to the idol of mobilization or distinctly subtracts from it. A critical theory can after all only be such, regardless of what its critical semantics convey, if it abandons its kinetic complicity with the movement of the world process into the worst of all possible directions. Thus it has to remain open if such a "third" critical theory can still exist not merely in name but in its full sense. If possible, it would put itself into effect at its outset as a pre-school of demobilization. Only as a still theory of movement, as a quiet theory of a loud mobilization, can a critique of modernity still differ from that which it critiques – all else is a rational cosmetics of participation, a conscious or unconscious nudging forward of already moving trains, a mimesis of the basic process within the process of reflection.

But it is impossible for such a "quiet" critique to generate its own beginning, its own jump out of the urge to act differently. The fact that it cannot do so is one of the riddles that are concealed in the ubiquitous post-modernist babble. Because whatever wishes to come after modernity would have to have gone through such a critique and have brought it to an end – no human being can claim that this is indeed the case with him in any significant way. All that can be said is that we have long begun to gain experience with the so-called "post-modern" passive voice and that it is not a very large step to admitting that we have, above all prospectively, landed on the suffering side of modernity. In this respect, the formula rings true: the more modern, the more post-modern. This is of great importance for the style of a "third" or post-modern critical theory, because in order to understand its own subject, it must have entered the modern scuffle without reservations – otherwise it would never arrive on the flip-side of things. But how this theory will find its way to something truly other from out of the modern Tempo-drome, that is something it will first have to explain – no, demonstrate – to us. The question of the possibility of an actually different "third" critical theory thus boils down to the classic riddle of how a quiet in the eye of the storm is possible for beings so thoroughly condemned to action.

One can now understand what it is exactly that the reminder of movement brings us – we get closer to an epistemological abyss where a theory without wisdom is no longer useful even as a theory. Should kinetics of all things become a school of serenity? We can hardly imagine what physicists and metaphysicists would have to say to that. Whatever their objections may be, this is where our entry into the investigation on the passive side of strong self-mobilizations ought to begin – an investigation into the process and progress of that which we have set in motion to speed over and past us. We ask, taking into account what happened, what it was that occurred so differently from what we planned. It turned out so very differently than expected, but what else could we have expected?

Sketches towards an Outline of a Critique of Political Kinetics

Why another critical theory of modernity? And why precisely now, at a time when most people have taken their lives beyond the reach of theories? And if there has to be a bare minimum of intellectual distance to the so-called "status quo," why not go with Marxism as usual? Why no recourse to the ethical potential of humanity? Why not poetry steeped in ruin at the Wailing Wall of facts? Or at least a fashionable skepticism towards the neoliberal swing of things? No, for the reason that Marxism, appeals to ethics, poetry, and skepticism of this kind are not in line with what is necessary and possible for critique because they themselves function at best as agents of impotent mobilizations and yet do not contribute enough to a fundamental understanding of mobilization events.

The fate of the Marxist social critique exemplifies this more than any other. In their time, Marx and his successors were of the partially justified opinion that they made the causes of modern radical changes in the world transparent with their analysis of capital flow. Additionally, they formulated a revolutionary ethics that saw the strategic core of its "praxis" in the political control over capital; from there, humanity's emancipation was rigorously to be steered towards a life in general wealth and limitless productivity. Thus, the fathers of socialism openly placed their bets on an ethics of productive mobilization with a humanistic intent. Admittedly, they did not suspect that only *one* aspect of their construction would be rather inadvertently realized, namely that regulatory instances must indeed be incorporated within or placed counter to capitalist processes if one is to prevent the worst for all of humanity. In more modern terms: without a certain, shall we say, "political" cybernetics of capital, the "host organism" that is earth, along with all its historic guests, is at the mercy of devastation. This cybernetics, should it ever come into play, stems in the long term less from socializations (since these alone lead to the effect of "more of the same, only worse") than from a consequent ecological curbing of production motives and the demilitarization of profits for the benefit of festive overspending in a general, mutual patronage.[8]

In its more assertive days, the old socialist Left tried to morally push its demand for political control over the processes of capital with the formula "socialism or barbarism" to the decision point. This is the point where its revolutionary politics fails when countered with actual historical findings, and the concept of world processes as mere effects of capital flows becomes consequently doubtful. Considering the results so far, very little can be found between barbarism and actual existing socialism to suggest mutual exclusion – however, there is a broad field of instances where they are synonymous. Now, it is a legitimate supposition that real socialisms not only had historic bad luck but also were unable to achieve anything better in a world full of enemies. Their mishap, however, is *also* caused by their fateful commitment to an inadequate concept of the modern kinetics of world change via Marxist analysis. Of course, it is not without reason that Marx saw his reconstruction of modern labor relations in capitalism as already having uncovered the *general* law of movement of modern class societies. Whatever it is that moves in these societies on a political, cultural, psychological, and ideological level, it can be, according to him, nothing more than a secondary movement that is determined in the last instance by the economic primary movement. This primary movement has exhibited a special legality since the eighteenth century, the age of the industrial revolution: since people's actions have been largely understood as "material reproductions of their lives" in the capital process, a categorically new phenomenon has emerged that no other age has had to contend with – the phenomenon of "work as such," the category of "work *sans phrase*." Marx sees this as the capture of human activities in the material life-process through the value creation of capital. The industrial proletariat gives the category of work *sans phrase* its social shape. But human activity only becomes "work as such" if it belongs to a form of production which in its very essence continually produces further possibilities of production. Marx explains this extraordinary phenomenon by linking the anthropological motive of self-production both to the economic motive of profit (i.e. investment return) and to the agonal motive of competition. An explosive mixture of motives emerges from the alliance between self-preserving self-sufficiency, pursuit of profit, and competition that lends the modernizing movement its impetus. The decisive mechanism in this new arrangement is indeed the suspected "self-exploitation of value" – that work of alchemy which organizes an activity in such a way that its result consists of the increase in ability to carry out the activity. Wherever the modern "work *sans phrase*" sets the rhythm, not only is a given form of life reproduced "economically" (in other words, in terms of home or palace economics), but also an increase in productivity becomes part of the primary product of production. This is precisely in accordance with the kinetic formula of mobilization. The self-exploitation of value as production of productivity is one of the many ways in which the modern mobilization loop begins to turn into movement that leads to more movement. Marx was right to describe capital which circulates around its own self-propagation as a demiurgic processing magnitude that forces the concrete lifelines of workers to march to its abstract rhythm for the sake of its self-sustaining self-propagation. But he gives far too little attention to the kinetic foundational process of modernity as the general movement towards more movement. Marx attributes the fact that "in modern times" everything moves further, faster, and more intensively to the dynamics of capitalist modes of production and uses confusing schemas of primary and secondary movement (i.e. base and superstructure) to interpret it as a problem that is *sui generis*. In reality, the capital process would never have begun if it had not been sustained by independent, parallel, and preceding structures of self-actualization and self-intensification. It is no coincidence that Marxist interpreters of early modern emerging movements continue to be perplexed by the riddle of "primitive accumulation." This perplexity necessarily remains as long as we insist on understanding the accumulation process in economic terms. In actual fact, the problem of accumulation leads to the core of modern kinetics, which is in turn – we've already said it – inseparable from the secret of subjectivity. We find more promising clues if we reject the question of primitive accumulation of capital and turn our attention to that of primitive accumulation of subjectivity – always provided that we are right to see it as not just a "metaphysical" phenomenon (which it also is in a certain sense) and not address it merely as the seat of intelligible and creative capacity, but above all to recognize the agency of self-movement towards movement in it, which is as puzzling as it is world-shaking. We would then be dealing with the primitive accumulation of a "kinetic energy" which – always mediated by subjective initiatives – repels itself from the world as first nature, turning it into pure raw material, energy source and substrate, which is then used by the kinetic energy to construct a New World from mobile artifacts on top of it. (In chapter 3, we will identify the nature of this kinetic subjectivity and connect it to the tension between a birth through a mother and a self-birth through one's own efforts.)

Wherever the modern kinetic model of success (movement towards increased mobility) begins to operate within a sector of activity, wayward contributions to the great dawn of the New World are created; a dawn where Europe is split off from its archaic, antiquated, and pre-modern way of being, followed by vast parts of the rest of the world. It is likely that classical Greece acted as a prelude to it: in sophistry, we can see the first signs of the development of intelligence into sport and in the Olympic games, a cult-like intensification of physical exercise. After that, the kinetic genie in a bottle seems to have been corked for a millennium and a half; it is only underground that the energies continued to rumble, having been exhausted in tribal feuds, migrations of peoples, Hunnish wars, Saxon slaughters, Germanic missions, politics of the first Reich, agriculture, livestock farming, monastic immersion, hermitage, simple reproduction. Then: the great initial spark. It seems to begin in the monasteries of the high Middle Ages, where the true factories of primitive accumulation of subjectivity are to be found. What is deployed here in the religious exercises of ascetic self-intensification – autogenic movement to increase movement, concentrating on concentration, immersing oneself in immersion, praying for work, working at being able to pray – has its analog in the various sectoral movements towards increasing self-powering mobility; in the accumulation of scientific knowledge which can only retain its status as valid knowledge if it is organized as research, that is, cognitive mobilization; in the self-exaltation of modern territorial states which soon reveal themselves to be transport states and arm themselves as nation states; in the dynamic of military mobilization, which has always been an arms race, that is, a battle for ballistic and kinetic advantages; in the self-dramatization of fit bodies that surrender to the ecstasy of increased movement almost as if entering a cult; in the self-erotization of sexual subjects who practice arousing their ability to be aroused; in the self-deification of the individual as artist, who revolves around the creation of their own creativity in a constant, expressive mobilization. In all of these fields and sectors of human mobility, self-mobilizations are being played out that span over several centuries, and the economic process is certainly their most willing medium, most unilateral driving force, and most versatile accomplice; in it, movement towards more movement pushes through industrial and monetary processes as well with an irresistibility that is *sui generis*. But the Marxian "value" that generates additional value per capitalization is in reality more a kinetic than an economic phenomenon; its parameter is the power to move, and its content, in turn, tantamount to being able to move.

A view of mobilization as a fundamental process of modernity has only recently been coming to light, not because anyone claims to be more insightful than the great social theorists of previous centuries but because the "thing itself" has appeared on the stage of recognizability for the naked eye to behold. It is only for us, in view of the late modern effects of acceleration, that the phenomenon of pure mobility has become real and conceivable. In analogy to Marx's vision of the *Fundamentals*, a categorically novel phenomenon seems to appear for the diagnosis of the late twentieth century: "mobility as such," "self-movement *sans phrase*." This postulates not only a third industrial revolution, with all that has been done to the reality of modern life by electronics, nuclear technology, and computer science, but also modern politics with its arms races, mass movements, and initiatives from above and below; it also assumes modern tourism and its conception of the world as service counter and landing strip; the cable-equipped screens, too, and the new disarray of love with its urban theater of separation, night clubs, computer games, and consoles in children's rooms; jogging in the park and athletic cults in the stadiums, disposable bottles, Andy Warhol's Factory, and the Captured Music... It is only once the self-movement *sans phrase* has directly forced its way into everyone's reality of life as a real category that the dynamic motif of a society made up of self-mobilizing subjects can be designated as such in the tone of calm critique without the diagnostician having to rise to the status of a prophet. And it is only recently that we have been forced to perceive in philosophical hindsight as well that Marx and Nietzsche said the same thing – the will to self-appropriating self-production and the will to power (as an initiative to enforce an interpretation of the world) are two alternate formulations of the same creative large-scale attack of the acting spirit on "matter," of the same kinetic nihilism that apprehends what exists as source of energy and construction site, nothing else.

We can differentiate three basic tendencies or categories of the modern fundamental process of mobilization, which has in the meantime absorbed the entire way of the world. The great self-movement towards more movement takes place first as a tendency towards motorization, installation of autonomous process units, and continuous acceleration of them ("tachocracy"); second, as a tendency to relieve, numb, and disable the functions of a subject that are too sensitive, slow, and oriented towards truth (automation through desensitization or elimination of context); third, through progressive eradication of distances and imponderables in coincidence with strategic appropriation of the other (logistics). In these three executing aggregates, the world as a hitherto inert resource for automobile system-subjects becomes processed, codified, made ready-to-use, and de-realized. De-realization is the psycho-social result of a systemic "self-realization" where the outdated term "reality" logically shrinks to the residual function of the not-yet-mobilized. For a few years now, American "deconstructionists" have been whispering the new message to each other: *there is nothing outside the text*;[9] only the naïve still cling to the antiquated fiction of the "external referent." Even epistemology shows glimpses of the impending short-circuit between kinetics and semiotics – the world is logically ripe for evaporation.

Only on the horizon of an omnipresent mobilization do we see that there can only be one kind of appropriate critique for such a reality that works towards a pervasive awareness of movement. Yet this is again formulated to be misunderstood, because this work towards awareness must not move forward but take a step back in order to gain distance and disconnect from the process of acceleration. Only hesitantly do we call the critical aspect of this mobilization theory after a classical model: the critique of political kinetics.

This critique claims the ugly and seemingly merely physical and subhuman concept of movement for the humanities, social sciences, and history in basic conceptual terms. We can only imagine what kind of reception the critique of political kinetics will receive when we recall what kinds of arguments and faces were made by the beautiful souls of the nineteenth century in response to the Marxist impertinence of accepting the term "work" as a fundamental category of historical anthropology. All we know is that this time the Marxists have joined the beautiful souls and bourgeois pragmatists as part of the great coalition of mobilizers: the Marxists because they are the first to understand that the critique of kinetics is only possible from a post-Marxist position that views "dialectical materialism" as just a particularly faded form of modern mobilization folklore; the beautiful souls because they are at least not inspired by such an ugly theory while they engage in their favorite occupation, the dawn of a New Age and the *Human Potential Movement*; the pragmatists because they in any case suppress any thought that could even remotely question their axiom of economic growth at a rate of 3% per annum.

Now, no one can be under the illusion that anything more can be called into question through a critique of political kinetics than just the growth rate of an industrial civilization that is racing – with the force of a train that's been accelerating for centuries – into the unknown. Whoever raises the question of kinetics does no less than to call into play the problem of whether and how this train can be brought to a halt, or at least diverted somehow. And it is a matter not of whether individuals can get off the train (of course they can, provided they are the right kind of individuals), but of whether modernity as a whole can free itself from a way of being that is ontologically determined by the formula "being-towards-movement."

These questions are too fundamental to be left to fundamentalists. Therefore, the critique of political kinetics exposes a working framework that can potentially be joined by every thinking and praxis that contributes in some way to the study of movement and to the exercise of the right kind of mobility. The critique of political kinetics will be a working title for the studies of a trans-disciplinary post-university "college." It can begin its exercises wherever the correctness of human and systemic movements needs to be examined. Like all other university-like entities, the trans-discipline for the awareness of movement requires power-neutral terrains to which the executives and stakeholders of the mobilizers have no access – it is the best tradition for the protection of theory since the European high Middle Ages. But since the operation of almost all currently active universities in this world has evolved into pre-schools of mobilization and cognitive subcontracting companies for the "attack of the present on the rest of all time," the critique of political kinetics has to look for other spaces in order to hold its studies. Whether this will take place in the New Social Movements, the centers for alternative culture, para-academic start-ups – that is not a pressing matter for the time being, and besides, these are also not the only possible alternatives. It is pressing, however, that the trans-discipline of the critique of movement cultivate polyvalent new brains of the societies in which the knowledge of demobilization from a variety of fields is instantiated. For all of us who come from the mobilization process, this knowledge will seem difficult to handle, implausible, and frustrating because the critique of political kinetics can under no circumstance be the theoretical conscience of a "praxis." Some will say that its bizarre and absurd result is to describe real processes in such a way that initially there is "nothing to do" – inasmuch as all those who are eager for action will make fools of themselves before doing what is to be done first, before hesitating, before stepping back to perceive more precisely, before ceasing with what has always been done, before imperceptibly becoming open to the correct movement. We can guarantee that anything else will once again yield blind mobilization, however magnificent the slogans of action may sound.

Though critique of political kinetics has its basic starting point in post-Marxism, we may not extrapolate that it relates to the insights of the socialist tradition in a destructive way. What carries weight compared to that tradition is the expansion of the conceptual field from production to mobilization, on the one hand, and the amendment of the prognostic symptoms of kinetics, on the other. One has to make the effort to once again study *The Communist Manifesto* in the way the text has for a long time now deserved to be studied: as the Magna Carta of aggressive kinetic nihilism, in which modernity declared for the first time what it is and what it wants. But a critique of kinetics will no longer be able to participate in Marx's euphoria in the face of the observation that in a world through which capital pulsates "all that is solid melts into air."[10] In this phrase, we can completely hear Marx as a thinker of mobilization – it is not for nothing that he has provided half the world with rationalizations for making history. But he is also a thinker of mobilization because his great terminology machine – especially the dialectic of productive forces and relations of production – is only built for the purpose of demonstrating the blastability of the inert conditions that still offer oppositions to the unleashing of effective production and the ultimate evaporation of assets. Marx's work-messianic vision is directed at a state of society where the activity of productive selves only has its own issues to deal with – removal of real resistance, total appropriation of the other, self-appropriating self-creation twenty-four hours a day. In its own way, a critique of political kinetics will indeed also know a "dialectic," namely that of the forces and conditions of movement; only it will not lament the fact that the conditions "still" inhibit the full use of the forces but rather dryly note, if need be, that the forces of movement are in any case not too far from "evaporating" all conditions in which conventional movements on our part have been possible. The critique of kinetics, too, will point out – in accordance with its derivation of post-modernism from the effects of a second passivity – that there is a growing organic compound of the masses of self-movement and therefore also a tendentious decline of the advantages of movement, but it would never occur to it to prognose a "revolutionary situation" from these observations; similarly, catastrophe-loving speculations about the connection between total system collapse and the rising up of the masses are foreign to it. What this critique does emphasize is nothing more or less than a crisis-induced opportunity for an evolutionary recall of the false mobilization forays.[11]

Just as the percentage of fixed capital permanently proportionally increases in the capital process, so too the dead automated centrifugal masses continuously swell in the world-wide mobilization of systems and increase their dominance over the gestures of living mobility to the point of oppression. Moreover, the same is true of the independent scientific research companies where the self-movement of theoretical apparatuses ensures that the act of thinking plays as good as no role in relation to what is thought. These extraordinarily uncanny operations are expressed by the concept of automation as inadequately as by the term "alienation" – our classical vocabulary is of no help to us whatsoever in the face of such new process-related realities. Movement is the great unthinkable in our languages.

Considering all of this, we can anticipate the contours of what a critique of political kinetics might entail. It does the groundwork for a critical theory of modernity that could use expressions of movement to describe how mobilization problematically sublates all Old World stock through mobilization and to criticize it through exercises in demobilization. There is no indication that something of this sort will be successful – except the success itself, for which it is impossible to decree any indubitable criteria. In any case, the point of departure for this critique is the observation that the departure of modernity towards an independent conscious life for all has largely lost itself in a rather blind kinetic passing on of the sometime initiated process congeries. The cost of the impressive yields of modern possibilities for self-movement and self-actualization in many fields is an incalculable and increasingly unbearable self-surrender to the subsequent automatic, self-lapsing processes. If we are right to imagine the immediate future as a time when the growing risks of disaster rapidly actualize, it is because we can already formulate the basic kinetic scheme of every possible accidental disaster: they will be the hetero-mobile result of countless self-mobilizations. A singular and dark inevitability emerges from the interaction between countless automatizations. And as concerns our much-vaunted future from a systemic point of view, its secret lies entirely in the variations of this great inevitability. Among these variations, we can determine two kinds of extremes: one leads to a relative cessation of mobilization as a whole via the mutual deceleration of partial processes (a great commendation to the obstacles?); the other drifts into the exponentiation of mobilizations through interactions to become an eco-kinetic inferno. And our process-consciousness? What role does it play in this world theater: that of the hero, the fool, or just a powerless audience member? If everything is really heading towards a fatal end, then our conscious self can take heart in the fact that it plays all the roles of the endgame at the same time so that it can be the audience of its own dramatic morphing from mobilization hero to process fool until the curtain falls. In the relatively benign version, on the other hand, subjects would be faced with a remarkable experience of themselves. In a time when modernity could save itself from itself, subjects, too, would stop moving as ontological agents of movement towards more movement. They would then know from their changed way of being that they are not the agents of mobilization but the "guardians" of real movement.

The Prospect of an Asian Renaissance: Towards a Theory of the Ancient

Wherever [the European] Mind prevails, there we witness the maximum of needs, the maximum of labor, capital and production, the maximum of ambition and power, the maximum transformation of external Nature, the maximum of relations and exchanges.

All these taken together are Europe, or the image of Europe.

Moreover, the source of this development, this astonishing superiority, is obviously the quality of the individual man, the average quality of *Homo europeus*. It is remarkable that the European is defined not by race, or language, or customs, but by his aims and the amplitude of his will.

Paul Valéry, "The European"[12]

It is an open secret among experts that for more than a hundred years now a large part of Western intelligence has been "Asianizing," as they say. Therein, one could perceive an ironic game that an object of cognition plays with its subject. In the world of intelligences, the discoverer is always exposed to a counter-discovery by those who have been discovered. For the bourgeois world between the seventeenth and nineteenth centuries, the interest in the East began under the sign of colonialism, which soon brought about an intellectual world trade. It was through the generation of early romantics that Asian imports were first brought to a theoretical level and incorporated into a generous synopsis of world cultures. A world conversation about world literature is what the cheerful mission statement of a romantic ecumenism proclaimed, in which Persian poetry and translations of the Upanishads were passed around as evidence of the actually metaphysical activity of the world soul.

But it did not end with philological flirtation. For the actual East, being discovered by another spirit turned out to be a date with destiny. What first began as discovery and then turned into conquest, mission, and instruction of the East soon pulled the old East into the mobilization of the planet along with it. Japan has given the world a model of self-liquidation in its final form, committing a seppuku for the sake of industry and history that will remain forever astonishing. Old Asia probably disappeared from the earth one day in the course of an epochal self-colonization, only surviving in the libraries of Western-inspired Indology, Sinology, Japanology, not unlike the way Old Europe has only survived in classical philology, medieval seminars, and period dramas.

This process must be formulated in an exaggerated way in order to correctly assess the Western Asian cult in all its strangeness. As the real East throws itself into industrial, scientific, political, and military mobilization in order to leave its old ways of thinking and being behind, the West is experiencing a cultural Asianizing for which there is no historical precedent – unless one wanted to accept the pervasion of the Roman Empire by Greco-Hellenic curricula as an analog. In this case, one would have to cite the cynical motif of conquering the conqueror; Horace's *Graecia capta ferocem victorem vincit* is still on the tip of the last humanists' tongues – after all, the verse ("Conquered Greece took prisoner her rough conqueror"[13]) proves how conspicuous it was even in a Roman setting to have a victor bow to the superiority of the vanquished.

Nevertheless, the *topos* of conquering the conqueror is not suitable for deciphering the inflation of Asianizing motifs in the current Western cultural scene. If we look through the historical arsenal for a prototype for current events, the only phenomenon that lives up to the occidental enthusiasm for Asia is that of a cultural renaissance.[14] We will argue in a moment that the phenomenon of "our" great Renaissance which occurred at the end of the Middle Ages can probably only be understood in light of today's Asia cult.

Renaissances are visualizations of old culture in a new context. A Renaissance shows its genius in finding the ability to step into something entirely unprecedented under the cover of its enthusiasm for a prominent antiquity. The unprecedented newness can emerge precisely by drawing inspiration from a great precedent – it seems as if enthusiastic repetitions are the great vehicle of innovation. In this way, Renaissances always owe their prolificacy to a passionate misunderstanding of the old by a newness that does yet not speak its name. Only through an intense misrecognition do antiquities get brought back to a new life – one that is not their own, but rather the fluorescence of the still necessarily self-misrecognizing current life.

What the Grecomania of the Italian Renaissance and then again of the late eighteenth and nineteenth centuries meant for the

self-forming of modern bourgeois society is by now culturo-histor-
ically evident. But what it might have to do with the more recent
Asiamania is still an unrevealed secret for most contemporaries
– many come to take this (certainly conspicuous) phenomenon to
be a fashion trend or an episodic exoticism. Thus, it would seem,
they make good use of their fundamental right to live in ignorance
of the major events of their time. But this does not change the
fact that things are being negotiated in the Asiamanic phenomena
of the present time which get to the heart of the world process,
insofar as we are able to know something about it. When the West
imagines itself to be in a sunken East and channels Asian antiquity
as a master model of culture for life in the present, it is searching
for possibilities of a future for itself within a foreign past. Nothing
other than this was precisely the case back in the great European
Renaissance, which rarely suspected the profound differences that
separated it from its ancient Greek models. Today's Asianizing
Renaissance similarly delves deep into old Eastern worlds of wisdom
to create pathways towards the new, the unprecedented, the inaccessible for late modernity, whose corruption seems threatening, if not
entirely incurable. For many, Asia is the cipher that offers shelter to
a concept of the inconceivable.

Initially, we can draw four conclusions from this. The first is
that a post-Christian era has begun within the Western hemisphere
that could not possibly find the terms it would require to understand itself within the scriptures of the Judeo-Christian tradition.
Following in the footsteps of the Young Hegelian Bruno Bauer, the
Young Conservative diagnostician Otto Petras already summarized
this situation in 1935 in the form of a still impressive intention
"to show that Christianity – the most formidable history-shaping
movement of our time – has exhausted its formative power and that
we live in a Post-Christianity understood in a deeper sense than the
calendar's AD."[15]

Secondly, modernity, thus left to its own devices – at least
according to the conviction of skeptical interpreters – has used up
its moral reserves and has no counterforces to deploy that could
intercept its own fatal drift. Enlightened secularism, with its dual
commitment to self-determination and large-scale technology, is
disappearing, it seems, before our very eyes in global neglect – things
run as they please and initial intentions are no longer of concern.
Thirdly, the attempts of the last Central European generations to
invoke livable forms of neopaganism from Germanic, Celtic, Greek,
and Latin religious antiquities have proved to be straw fires that
sometimes burned off with barbaric fumes and rarely on a level
higher than that of spiritual party conversations. Thus, anyone who

is interested likely knows that under present conditions one might perhaps make a rural commune with that homemade raw substance of Old European and pre-Christian elements, but no longer a territorial state. Fourth, a turn to the East (for Americans, it is not a turn anyway, but a continuation on their old Western course, only through water) brings into play no less than a world-cultural alternative to the Greco-Judeo-Christian path that retains its quality as alternative even when the actual contemporary Eastern hemisphere modernizes itself beyond recognition by adopting Western mobilization techniques.

What does it indicate that in the crisis of late modern Western world this phenomenon – here referred to as an Asian renaissance – is interlaced with it? If a logic of the Renaissance really exists, then the new Asiamania should be read as a sign that creative members of post-Christian civilization hope to come to an understanding of themselves by grasping at antiquity once again – but this time not so that it can be appropriated as one's *own* antiquity, but as antiquity in a foreign form. This time, the illusion of a "memory" of something that once belonged to us is not being sought. Today, an Asian antiquity rising to the rank of exemplarity has to do not with what is foreign or one's own, but with the very spirit of the ancient as such. In other words, we have become so uncanny to ourselves through our modernization that the old, strange sounds of the Far East suddenly begin to sound like an old, familiar idiom. And although it is obviously not a native language that touches us so suggestively in this respect, it could – after many twists and turns – become a sister language to the mother tongue. To put it differently, once again: the destruction of our own traditions by way of modern analytics has stripped our lives down to the stumps – that is, all the way down to the anonymous awareness of the fact that we find ourselves in a world that is both foreign and our own at the same time. This design-making awareness that is thrown into being can now learn the language of Buddha as well as that of Plato in order to clarify its strange position to itself insofar as it experiences every language as a foreign one. From now on, it only knows itself as that which cannot know itself and cannot name itself – and if it can, then only in the form of a persistent self-misrecognizing, of an essential theatricality. From the anonymousness of this existence, the path to Lao Tzu or Chuang Tzu is no longer than the path to Parmenides or Augustine, the ascent to Plotin and Hegel no steeper than the one to Nagarjuna and Shankara, the path through Aristotle no drier than the one through Patanjali, the entry into the way of being of Meister Eckhardt no more mysterious than that of Master Dogen. Whether of Eastern or Western origin, the same exhausting improbability looms over these old names and doctrines, the same fascinating strangeness. Precisely because modernization has evaporated our Old European traditions and identities by way of progressive mobilization, the most foreign ancient tradition is no longer more foreign than the one that has until recently been our own.

It is in this context that the punchline of the Asian Renaissance in the modern West becomes clear: it makes us so pointedly aware of the question of the ancient preconditions of the modern enterprise that while we can underestimate, misunderstand, combat, and disregard it, we can in the end no longer shake it off. As long as these times remain modern, they will be haunted by the question of the compatibility of human life processes and modernity itself. Since human culture is demonstrably very old and modernity very new and unsubstantiated, it is not a secondary task to find out if modernity is an outdoing of the ancient by the means of the modern or if its modernity puts a final end to antiquity. This question has become so urgent that the difference between the familiar and the foreign no longer plays any major role in these matters. Since the most foreign traditions are no longer more foreign to us than our own, it becomes clear how much our path towards the unparalleled has put *all* of the Old World nature and culture reserves up for negotiation. Because it is by now undeniable that a universalizing modernity exists in the form of "mobilization as such," the question of "antiquity as such" pushes itself to the forefront almost violently. Then what is it that we take with us from antiquity on our trip into the unprecedented? Which dowries from the ancient world still create a link between past and future? What provisions will future generations live on during their continued exodus? How do the vessels in modern outer space stay in contact with the ancient ground controls?

These very questions indicate that the Asianizing Renaissance goes far beyond the events of the Grecizing Renaissance in the early bourgeois mobilization time; it is both more than and different from a mere cultural quote that will unleash something unprecedented in allusion to an authentic antiquity. Because it already emerges *after* this unleashing and already has an impression of what modernity can be, it poses the question more radically than the Renaissance of the fifteenth and sixteenth centuries and seeks the ancient as something that is not just as a pretext for the modern. Since the world belongs to the moderns anyway, the moment has come to inquire about the possibility of the ancient as ancient. Modern Asiamania is a Renaissance to the extent that it sides with those antiquities – whether ancient culture or nature – that create conditions for New World adventures. Thus, the new Asiamanically encrypted "Renaissance as such" asserts the authority of the ancient in two ways: on the one hand, it stresses that modernity would not exist if it could not – as user and consumer of pre-modern resources – depend on that which it (in an ultimately self-destructive way) exploits without regenerating; on the other hand, it proves that the New World enterprise fundamentally overwhelms the ancient precepts since modernity follows the drive to carry out an infinite project on a finite basis. It obeys this drive if it has constituted itself metaphysically as being-towards-movement. This is actualized through us in the production of expanded productivity, in the will to a further reaching will, in the imagining of heightened imagination, in the creation of more comprehensive creativity, in short, in the movement towards movement *ad inifinitum*. As being-towards-movement, modernity is defined as "mobilization as such," in other words as being-towards-self-annihilation.

The "Renaissance as such" that we see at work in the Asianizing activity of the more sensible West equals nothing less than an ontological sign change.

For if there is a common denominator for the currents of ancient Asian thought, it is that they grasp the meaning of being as a being-towards-stillness-within-movement. Even where, as in yoga, one works with the highest mobilizations of forces in the sense of a mystical physiology, the focus of consciousness is always on the advancement towards stillness within strength. The Asianizing tendencies in the West are perhaps only awkward tentative attempts in this direction – they express the intuition that nothing less than an ontological sign change will suffice to take the fatal thrust out of the "processes of modernization." Nowadays, whoever looks for a language of demobilization will most likely find it in the ancient Eastern realm, where different dramaturgies have been developed for the kinetics of the will to live than in the Western mobilization civilization. And it is only by borrowing from such languages, which irritate us with their frustrating wisdom, that it is possible to point, however awkwardly, to what needs to be said in the midst of the worldwide movement towards movement. The unthinkable impertinence that is heard by modern ears in old Asian "quietist" keys is aimed at the kinetic demission of mobilizing systems and subjects. But can we seriously imagine our de-automobilization? Can we conceive of a way of being where the system-subjects would no longer be driven forward by their self-advancement propellers? Does a prospect even exist for us where the powers of the subject generate something other than otherworldly acceleration, enrichment, research, and empowerment?

These questions do not comprise disclaimers for modernity after-the-fact owing to bad experiences with it. They are as old as modernity itself; indeed they are inseparable from the superb upswing of early Romanticism, in which an offensive modernism, sustained by the élan of self-outdoing, inquired beyond itself in its best philosophical moments. Novalis' phrase – "One is greatly in error if one believes that antiquities exist. Antiquity is only now coming into being"[16] – already holds the key to the post-modern Renaissances. What emerges out of the new antiquities are shadows that belong to the light of modernity. The more modern, the more post-modern – there is no way around this formula. Aside from an imperceptible boundary, nothing can survive the impulse of modern self-mobilization *ad infinitum* unchanged unless it be through the boundless generosity of post-modern patronage for the benefit of "Renaissances" as such.

2

THE OTHER CHANGE: ON THE PHILOSOPHICAL SITUATION OF ALTERNATIVE MOVEMENTS

... one man is a fool – two are a new humanity!
Robert Musil, *The Enthusiasts*[1]

Every age has its own style of being dissatisfied with the world. And every dissatisfaction that becomes self-conscious contains within itself the seeds of a culture.

Today's dissatisfaction with the world shows unmistakable traits of panic. Those who do not sense the panic are not up to speed – presumably they live off-site, in an asynchronous cave, having been spared, sparing themselves any exertion, living on a private income, perhaps happy as well, transported into a province out of reach from the news. To avoid panic, one would have to trust one's small good fortune. One would have to have the old psychological immune system that uses immediate worries to protect itself from big questions. But immunity to panic is rare nowadays, as is any believable unworldliness. Whoever reads the newspaper and eats mushrooms is already contaminated. Even those who are constructive-minded can get no further than a little bit of positivity against a panicked background. Goodwill no longer has a common denominator with the course of the world.

All of this says that panic is not a symptom of mass hysteria, nor does it present a personal case of the nerves. Speaking in classical terms, it is a constitution of the objective spirit, articulating an adequate relationship of the intellect to the matters at hand, and should the spirit lose its composure at what it discovers, it is right in this matter. It is the same with the panicked spirit as it is with Lessing's Father Galotti: if you don't lose your mind over some things, you have no mind to lose. Panic proves to be the obligatory way of being of a consciousness that delves into its time – into our time. And that is why panic cannot be adopted or discarded like an external code, the possibility of inciting or appeasing it being illusory; its very nature is to be beyond manipulation because it is older than all calculation – ultimately, panic is not born of scaremongering but the other way around.

In panic, we discover a fundamental feature of the truth about the present historical moment, and even more so an aspect of the truth about the brittle historicity of contemporary existence. If we are gripped by panic, then it has become clear to us that historical time dies with us – in such a way that at its end, barely anything will have happened. Our history – all that we are and have – will one not too distant day not have anyone for whom it is something that has happened. That is why panic arises – and insofar as it arises, it is the intelligent tinge of the moment in which we realize how time trickles away for us into the realm of might-as-well-never-have-been. Something would only have happened to us if a future exists that retains its past – our present – as its origin. Such retention has been the great work of the civilizational imagination which ensured that what has been "remain as happened." To remain as having happened means to enter into memories. But since we cannot rule out the absence of a future that remembers us, panic seeps into the signature of the present time as an inevitable feature of it. Before the panicked world-view, the entire historical context disintegrates and the usual impermanence of things suddenly turns into a panicked impermanence. It is as if a black hole appeared in time into which all that has happened within time disappears. Vertigo in the background, a tear in the film of representations, a flavor of unreality and emptiness – and panic is the form in which the end-times are "there" for the insightful zeitgeist from now on. Put simply, panic is the post-Christian, neo-pagan version of the apocalypse; it arrives at the same time as the re-actualization of Greek motifs from the ancient fund and occupies the space left open by the receding Judeo-Christian interpretations of the last things. Ever since time has run out for historical messianism, the bell of panicked worldly experience has tolled once more.

This explains why today's style of dissatisfaction with the world can be nothing other than a panicked one. What is not explained, however, is whether a panicked consciousness that pushed through to self-affirmation could be the stylistic principle of a post-Christian culture. Even less is said about the question of whether the movements that present themselves as alternatives contain enough mental substance and lifestyle to bring about an alternative culture from their new attitude to the world in which the attitudes to life and interpretations of being human would take shape for the coming millennium. Only one thing is certain: the macabre undertone in the phrase "panicked culture" is not without reason.[2]

This undertone not only insinuates the shift from religious apocalypse to post-religious panic, but it also foreshadows with an uncomfortable realism the coming era as a kind of earthly purgatory where sinners who can still be rescued must undergo dire courses of treatment. For one can only describe the due learning processes of the kind found at the level of great social and political systems in terms of a diabolical autodidacticism. In this view, the historically moved planet appears to be something between hell and adult education, where the poor souls have to memorize the conditions for their own survival through a disastrous self-study.

In connection with these scandalous reflections, we engage those employed at the alternative front in a historical conversation. Why? Because it must be shown how the most militant dissatisfactions with the actual have a share in a very old history of dissatisfaction with the state of earthly affairs. The current alternatives are to some extent the partners and to some extent the heirs of epochal alternative movements whose beginnings date back to the "rise" of advanced civilizations. Consequently, today we are dealing not only with trivial efforts to reform bad global conditions such as fill the history books, but also with a completely newly constructed and organized alternative to a previous alternative movement. Ecologists, autonomists, fundamentalists, the neo-religious, Green pacifists – all of them get caught up in a very distant history of revolts and revolutions, where an older dissatisfaction with the world has already created its classical expression of it. To positively define the philosophical locus of today's alternatives, we must distinguish between two kinds of alternativity: the first (or metaphysical) type of disagreement with the world, which aims for transcendent beyond-worlds or utopian counter-worlds; and the second (or poetic) type of disagreement with the world, which sees the track that shows the way out in reality itself.

Panicked Culture – or: How Much Catastrophe Does a Person Need?

Let us begin with a succinct thesis: today's alternatives are already the children of catastrophe. What differentiates them from earlier generations and makes them the most likely candidates for a panicked culture is their expert-like approach to the potential disasters that surround them. From a historical perspective, the alternatives are likely the first humans to cultivate a non-hysterical relationship to a possible apocalypse. For the first time ever, we do not have to imagine doomsday scenarios to see the writing on the wall. The current situation takes care of that sufficiently. Nowadays, the apocalypse calls attention to itself as if its name were in lights on Broadway. With dry professionalism, it writes its own letter of announcement. Apocalyptic alarm no longer presupposes religious uproar; warnings of the end-times do not imply that prophetic individuals have declared themselves to be the mouthpiece of transcendent revelations. The current alternative consciousness is characterized by what we might call a pragmatic attitude towards catastrophe. The catastrophic is now a category that no longer belongs to visions but to perception. Nowadays, anyone can be a prophet if they dare to say anything at all. In any case, catastrophe needs less an announcement than a transcript – linguistically, its place is not among apocalyptic promises but among the daily news and committee reports. The writing on the wall appears in ordinary language and the only thing that belongs to modern doomsday prophesies (aside from a spray can) is empirical data, such as that pertaining to the events of the year 1986, which has already attained symbolic features with its series of fatal accidents.

What can the expression "panicked culture" mean? Does panicked experience even allow for culture? To the extent that culture must be built upon expectations, repetitions, certainties, and institutions, does it not presume the lack, indeed the exclusion, of the element of panic? We vote for the opposite to be the case. It is only through proximity to panicked experiences that living cultures are possible – it is only the occasional experience of the extreme that exposes the temperate human region where we can cultivate what we are competent to do. One of the attributes of the Greek Pan was to be the god of the midday hour when the shadows are at their shortest and the world is dashed to the ground by light, holding its breath in his presence. The modern term "panic" forgets this connection between presence, revelation, and fright – the only thing it remembers is the kinetic motif of directionless escape. Above all, it no longer knows what is most important: bearable human life is always an island within the unbearable, and the existence of islanders is only ensured through the discretion of a subtly present ocean. The world that we are assured of is thus always placed against an either (Judeo-Christian) apocalyptic or (pagan) panicked background. But modernity wants presence without tears. It sees culture only as a state of being where the existence of faucets answers the question about the origin of water, just as the problem of the origin of "truth" is taken care of through the dealings of scholars. A panicked culture would be immediately recognized by its respect for faucets; after all, it is possible that when you turn one on, the ocean comes out. It would be no different with the sciences, especially since they have been generating things for a long time now under which the world has the same right to cower as humans and animals once did under the panicked Greek light of midday.

A few questions are now inevitable. Does alternative culture then need catastrophe? Does it secretly approve of disasters, as people sometimes fear to be the case? Does it have to be addicted to calamity because only this creates a climate where alternative ideas gain popularity? Is catastrophe essential for the introduction of a new movement, like a teacher who eventually convinces even the most stubborn minds of his or her lessons? Do humans need catastrophe because they must be educated and can only be educated by the school of worst possible scenarios? Consequently, are the real hopes of alternative movements not linked to disaster-didactic calculations – provided it is true that only a visual instruction of the worst can usher in a turn for the better?

It was in the days of the Harrisburg nuclear accident on Three Mile Island in 1979 that I really understood what disaster didactics meant for the first time. As the out-of-control reactor boiled and everyone held their breath to see if this infernal machine would explode, I noticed an uncanny phenomenon in myself and in others. Of course, no one could have any doubt about the devastation that an explosion of the nuclear reactor could cause, nor could anyone guarantee that what seemed to be a safe distance from accidents of this kind was actually safe. And yet at the time of Harrisburg, there was an option in the air *in favor* of the catastrophe; one could sense a sly sympathy with the explosive substances in the reactor casing. It was as if the deadly radioactive substances not only represented a physical quantity, but also contained a culturally critical message that deserved to be released. The small, immoralist neurosis in the face of the defective nuclear reactor was therefore not just a milieu-specific perversity, not just a sign of pyromania or evidence of an inclination towards the macabre within the human nervous system that is characterized by ever stronger stimuli to gain arousal. In it, a whole way of thinking came to light together with its dubiousness. Within its own logic, the option for the explosion was nothing more than an educational hypothesis about the didactic and mind-changing energies that radiate from *actually occurring* disasters.

Only through Chernobyl did the underlying disaster-pedagogical implications of Harrisburg come to light. Indeed, if the worst has to occur before relearning can begin, then, from this perspective, the Harrisburg incident was "not bad enough." Because the big explosion failed to materialize, the Harrisburg disaster could not reach the level where disaster didactics develops its grim calculations. It is the level where one believes that compelling connections between misfortune and insight can be formed. According to this dicey logic, such connections arise through an absurdly magnified application of the basic idea that those who do not listen will have to learn the hard way. In fact, disaster-pedagogical thinking promises that even the greatest calamity can be referred to a human scale – that is, into the field of sensible measures for preventing its repetition – through subsequent learning. Consequently, after Harrisburg, the term "warning disaster" made a career for itself in the vocabulary of alternative movements – a term that encapsulates the hope that disasters might penetrate our otherwise unteachable minds like probes and ignite new insights within them.[3]

This desperate theory of learning shines a light on the state of the enterprise that has been calling itself Enlightenment since the eighteenth century. It began as a utopia of an unforced guidance towards better understanding. By using the soft logic of an autonomous thinking that listens to the "voice of reason," it wanted to eliminate the violence that cuts deep when it comes to learning the hard way. In the meantime, however, even the well-meaning old Enlighteners are not very far from adding disaster to the curriculum of humanity as the last pedagogical tool, if it is really the only way that something can still be learned. Thus, we can see how classical Enlightenment, with its concept of truth based on argumentation, has been pitifully put on the defensive. No one seriously believes that something essential can still be reached on the path of listening. "Let learning the hard way be welcome; for listening has failed."[4] There are more than a few tireless members of the old Enlightenment troop who are already at the point of being glad if at least one treatment of learning the hard way in the face of disasters that cut deep could contribute a little bit to the establishment of truth in the "civilizing process" at the very last moment (oh, this word that burns the tongue!). And thus emerges the strange affective pull towards *actually occurring* doom. The catastrophe will show *them*! The real present calamity apparently closes the gap between argument and disclosure, bridging the distance between the appeal to the imaginative consciousness and its overpowering with existing evidence. The catastrophe is thus the apt reversal of a miracle – no wonder, and why is it not one? Because it is a direct consequence of what the deluded activists are up to. The real present catastrophe thus attains a formidable truth-theoretical function: it complements the mere argument and brings massively into presence what can otherwise only be imagined. By bridging the evidence gap between listening and learning the hard way, the didactic catastrophe places the epiphanic truth of an event above the discursive truth of the imagination. And thus the problem of learning from disasters leads to the logical center of enlightenment and modernity. Modernity is, after all, the enterprise where human intelligence is not content with just giving voice to right pronouncements about the world; it can only be satisfied if it has actively ensured that the right things happen to the world as a whole. But this active concern for what is right is in the most radical crisis. For if now even human-made catastrophe ought to impose a tax on learning how to do things right, then it is a fatal testament to the way that modernity has strayed from its conception of learnable right action under the guidance of success and truth.[5]

The hope for a way to learn from the worst thing at the very last minute is difficult to distinguish from despair about the possibility of learning at all.

Four brief comments will illustrate the risks and limitations of disaster-didactic thinking below. It is only from the failure of this desperate learning theory that the reason why alternative cultures will only be possible as a panicked culture becomes plausible. These observations are commentary on the question that is on the lips of every contemporary: what more needs to happen before something happens? Practically oriented, it could also say: how big would a catastrophe need to get before it radiates the universal flash of insight that we are waiting for? From what point on would disasters be the self-evident grounds for radical mentality-changing insights? How bad does it have to get before it can get any better? Does it have to get bad at all? Does the underlying link between misfortune and insight have validity?

It is clear from the very first remark how problematic an answer to these questions would be, indeed how problematic the questions themselves are already. Clearly, there is no *quantitative* measure that could be adopted as the "didactically" sufficient size of the disaster. In various ways, the conscious minds of humans have the ability to stay immune to disastrous evidence. Presumably, the silent majority always stays outside the possible radius of damage of great disasters. Additionally, the citizens of the modern epoch have long experienced their era as a fateful event that cannot be mapped onto any reasonable will. The second fatalism that is dawning on all sides belongs to an awareness that realizes the extent to which things already occur differently than one might think. Moreover, the most powerful groups of modern societies have politically, ideologically, entrepreneurially, and vitally invested so much in the most dangerous mobilization techniques that even accidents on the largest scale must not cause any doubts on grounds of principle about the course and speed of the civilizing process. In these circles, mentalities exist that are irreversibly, extremely set on mobilization; in the bunker of their automatic responses, they can hold their own against any agitation. Even evidence of actual disaster ricochets off such structures. For them, revelation does not take place. In the end, minds are tougher than facts, and those who did not want to listen when it was still possible will also make themselves immune to learning the hard way, too.

If these considerations are true, then the insinuation that Harrisburg was not yet bad enough to learn anything decisive from becomes doubly transparent in its questionability. Obviously, catastrophe is conceived here as a quantum which, according to allopathic principles, produces stronger effects at higher dosages. With this logic, we immediately get into the most uncomfortable escalation. The victims of Chernobyl will have been lying in terrible agonies for a long time when a zealous didactics announces itself and says: Chernobyl was not terrible enough either, because, after all, the International Organization of Soldiering On is holding it together more determinedly than ever. The relentless consequence of this can only be that more has to happen – but to what extent?

The pedagogization of disaster eventually also fails because of an aesthetic subversion. Since metaphysical or moral meanings for major accidents are no longer available to us in the modern age, images of disaster can no longer be easily provided with a moral key. To the extent that the "readability" of catastrophes ends, their phenomenal and aesthetic visibility is revealed. On the day after the *Challenger* disaster in 1986, I was giving a lecture on the criteria of post-modern aesthetics at the Academy of Art in Karlsruhe which was followed by a discussion with the audience. There, a not so young student in a black shirt and grey hat spoke up and declared almost triumphantly that he had enjoyed the televised images of the exploding rocket. Hearing that confession, I stood there for a moment, speechless – you are suddenly in the eye of the storm, knowing that this was said from within the core of modern kinesthetics where the world is spun into a series of "images." With such memories, you remain skeptical towards the prospect of epiphany through disaster evidence. In the best-case scenario, a demonic Kantianism would emerge, which would transfer the concept of the sublime from *The Critique of Judgment* to reactor explosions and the view of biologically dead oceans.

The second remark on disaster didactics connects to the *topos* of "learning through mistakes," wherein humanity's oldest theory of learning is stored. It contains the insight that only a child who has had a burn can understand fire. Because intelligence is not a theoretical quantity but represents a behavioral quality of creatures in an open environment, it must go through the school of fire. Without experiencing burns, you have no idea how to cope with life. The world is not always good and does not tolerate all kinds of behavior. A warning pain must be engraved in the nervous system in order to reliably embody the selectivity predetermined by the world. Human wisdom has been bound to the engrams of suffering from time immemorial. Thereby, disaster-didactic thinking seems initially justified, because it is based on the assumption that humanity make sense of nuclear damage in an epoch-spanning learning process. This sense-making would be identical to the act we are facing in the "drama of the history of species." Because humanity enters its path into the unprecedented as a student without a teacher, it would have to teach itself what it cannot learn from anyone else. It must endure being fated to an auto-didactics as a matter of life and death. Its goal of study sounds like a fairytale: it is supposed to transform itself through its own power from a coercive community of deadly stupidity into an ecumenism of intelligences. Evidently, outrageous demands are being made of its auto-didactic genius. In a study of itself that involves many victims, we will see if humanity can teach itself about itself and its planetary situation, or if it still proves to be a learning-impaired subject.

The question of the learning ability of our species touches on a critical point: humanity is *a priori* learning impaired because it is not a subject, but an aggregate. When we speak of humanity, we are creating a general term that can only haunt speculative sentences in the form of an allegorical subject – sentences that the Age of Enlightenment made carefree use of. What appears to be a crisis of enlightenment universalism today is in fact a transition from the study of humanistic allegories of the species to that of a hard ecology of local intelligences. This ecology begins only after the completed insight that humanity has no self, no intellectual coherence, no reliable organ of wakefulness, no self-reflection capable of learning, no identity-building common memory.[6]

That is why humanity cannot be wiser than a single human being – indeed, even as a whole it cannot become as wise as an individual who has learned the hard way. The aggregate we call humanity has no body of its own with which to learn the hard way – no hand by which to learn first-hand – but rather a foreign body, its place of residence, the earth, which does not become wise, but transforms into a desert. The classic model of learning from harm collapses before this fact. All future learning processes at the level of the species will be fraught with an almost intractable problem of transmission: the question of how acquired and embodied intelligence can be transferred from one who has become wise to the unwise; more generally speaking, how individual insights can be incorporated into social institutions and technical systems. Only individuals can be wise; institutions are well designed, at best.

The third remark concerns itself not with the subjectlessness of "humanity," but the subjectlessness of disaster – if I may use this manner of speaking. Our everyday understanding shows an inkling of this when it follows its usual habit of interpreting great disasters in a fatalistic way. We think of fatality under the schema of the anonymous event. In contrast, it is crucial for disaster didactics to view even the most massive disaster under the schema of personal action. Disaster as event does not have the same grammar as disaster as action. Of the first, we say: *it* happened, *it* fell upon us. Of the second: *someone* did it, *someone* let it get to this point. It is only when the disaster has a subject – you could also say a culprit – that it makes sense to interpret it as a stimulus for self-critical relearning. In order for learning to become possible after disasters, a subject must be assumed that sees the disaster as *their own* and refers to it as their own deed.

Only disasters that are "committed" by someone can form this arc of reflection which confronts the perpetrator with themselves while bypassing the event. It is only disaster as action that creates this recourse which presents the seemingly impersonal calamity to a particular subject as their previously hidden "true reality." Understanding the disaster therefore means setting in motion a kind of oedipal investigation: only insofar as the disaster that happened is an indirect crime does the investigation expect metanoia, rethinking, and repentance from an unconscious or hybrid perpetrator. Thus, here, as in any thinking that judges morally, both the interpretation of the event as deed and the identifying of a culprit are indispensable.

It remains questionable, however, if an accident like that of Chernobyl can be attributed to an offender. Aside from the operational aspects and general breakdown risks, isn't Chernobyl also a result of epistemological and socio-cultural developments in an anonymous and unattributable way, which build upon premises that are thousands of years old and lead to nuclear technology? Is it still possible to seek culprits and assign responsibility in processes of this scale? It would be justified if it could be shown that this entire development is an occurrence where the occidental type of human theoretically works out their unmistakably peculiar will, realizes it technocratically, and enforces it in the form of a planetary politics that enslaves nature. The perpetrator could then be identified as the subject of a Western culture of will and understanding, and traced back to every single citizen of modernity, provided that each of us is made up of an objective complicity with this imperialist, nature-consuming ego. All those who participate in modernity would thus be members of its primordial horde that is bound together by the collective crime of matricide.

Let us assume for a moment that it could act the way that this speculation presumes. Don't we have to break off the investigation and follow the modern culprit-self into the fate of its self-becoming? What has awakened the will to dominate nature in this culprit? Who or what gave the culprit the weapons to do their deed? What history could in the end turn this dominant subject into a master of nuclear fire as well? How was the will for domination positioned within it, and what instances of takeover provided access to exactly this desire and this ability? Is a compulsion to desire perhaps prior to this will to power? Is a certain formation of a self by its very nature as disastrous as a nuclear reactor explosion? Does this self that has attained the power to destroy nature not also happen to "itself" like an anonymous disaster? And is this why the potent agency and ability of modernity relates to itself as suffering and powerlessness?

These questions are being asked to show that even disasters that have been "committed" can ultimately never fit into the context of deed and doer. In them, the boundary that separates the logic of responsible action from the logic of the tragic act is crossed. In the tragic deed, not only is the offense the product of the perpetrator, but the perpetrator themselves is the result of what happened. The dramatic-tragic consciousness crystallizes only at the event itself and no "learning process" follows because the tragic deed makes it clear that the disaster and its perpetrator are made of the same substance. Thus, Chernobyl could belong to the tragedy of ability and desire, where the doers and their disaster emerge from the same happening – from the history of cognitive mobilization of the subject and the planet.

The fourth remark pertains to the relationship between truth and disaster itself. If disaster didactics sheds a light on the agony of the Enlightenment, then an agony of truth is simultaneously at play. In fact, the idea that disaster "reveals something" is only so suggestive to us because we have always associated revelation – in Greek, apocalypse – with truth. Truth – insofar as it "appears" – has ever been presented as a coming-to-light or being evident. In this respect, every kind of enlightenment contains a drama of light or illumination – without this photological element, we would not know what knowledge means at all and why it is always the bright side of things that faces in the direction of knowledge. If, for us, the possibility of a realization of "truth" is tied to the coming to light of previously dark things, then the younger Enlightenment as light-emitting process has also made extensive investments in this lighting model of truth.

But we are witnessing the death throes of truth. The old alliance between light and truth – the photological pact of occidental rationality – has been torn ever since we have been able to use what gives light to bring death. Nuclear weapons also make philosophical history. From a photological point of view, truth takes place as an event of exposure on a three-step scale: it increases from a natural or artificial lighting of dense bodies that become visible through their self-sufficient reflection to an active and invasive fluoroscopy of the bodies until the bodies are finally transformed entirely into light. The photological Enlightenment encompasses all and any objects from the point of view of their luminosity, transparency, transformability into light. If Enlightenment has a dramatic finality in itself, it is located in the eradication of the initial difference between light and matter as it appears in ordinary lighting via a terminal transformation of all matter into light. As long as Enlightenment operated in the middle (analytical) stage of an X-Ray logic, it could not foresee the end of its movement towards light – the light-kinetic dimension of the process only became transparent in the moment that modern nuclear physics actually reached the level of a radical thinning of matter. The cutting-edge technologies under the rule of light are a consequence of the photological process in that they turn matter directly into "light" – brighter than a thousand suns. But what can we still see in this light? Is the light of a nuclear explosion one in which the world would learn something about its situation? Or does not this light itself turn into the last reality, into the disappearance of everything in a lightstorm? Instead of shedding light on the state of things, the thinning light eliminates them, together with those who wanted to understand them.

Something of these paradoxes takes effect in the speculations of disaster didactics as well. Those who count on learning from disaster expect the explosion to illuminate dark minds. The warning disaster is itself supposed to be the disaster warning. The actually occurring transformation into light is supposed to critically examine our civilizational process. Those who follow this logic to its conclusion will arrive at a fatal conclusion: only an apocalypse could act as a convincing warning against an apocalypse. Only an actual disaster could provide evidence for a truth that must occur both apocalyptically and in the present in order to become completely true. Thus, the only disaster that makes sense to all is a disaster no one survives.

When all of the possibilities to transform disaster into pedagogy are played out and have been understood in the context of their necessary failure, then all the pathways for the history-making reflex of fleeing forward will be blocked. The powers that produce the catastrophe and at the same time want to be saved from it suddenly pile up on top of themselves. It is not "Save yourself if you can!" but "Recognize the situation!" that becomes the slogan of the age. And thus the situation emerges where panicked consciousness could develop into culture. Everything before that point remains the bourgeoisie with rocket ships. It is only through the experience of panic that one is freed from didactic illusions – it is the bridge to a consciousness that no longer hopes to gain something from disaster, certainly no civilization-critical revelations. Panicked culture begins where mobilization in the form of a permanent flight forward ends. For this reason, the "history" of a panicked culture would play the role of the chronic end of history itself – the kinetic motives that have heretofore made history would be tamed in it by way of an explicit culture whose efforts would be to prevent the invasion of new history-making impulses from precisely the post-historic knowledge of the catastrophe of historical mobilization. This, a previously esoteric form of consciousness (referred to as enlightenment within spiritual jargon), would become a public matter. In a panicked-ecstatic culture, entire populations would perform an act that was previously only done by a scattered few: the leap of consciousness through time to the end-times and the subject's exit from the causality of flight and hope. Thereby, the post-historical culture of panic would be the only alternative to the culture of historical mobilization, which already has no more history left ahead of it – just a countdown.

The First Alternative: Metaphysics

Alternative cultures come into existence when humans find themselves in an irrevocable disagreement with the world. For this reason, today's individuals with an alternative view cannot be seen as the inventors of the alternative. They are not the first ones to have their discontent with the world become confident and fundamental. In order to understand the meaning of alternative culture in a more radical sense, we must dig around in the submerged layers of our tradition of ideas. If we go back a few millennia, the archeological dig for traces of an old protest against the world will make a find. There, we encounter sediments containing the beginnings of high forms of religion and metaphysical interpretations of the world. What metaphysics presents as a philosophical phenomenon is not up for discussion; so too, its basic conceptual structures and the variants of its architectonics are of no concern to us at this moment. Metaphysical statements made by humans are only of interest to us insofar as a crucial chapter in the prehistory of discontent with the world connects to their emergence. We interpret the appearance of metaphysical forms of thought as an indication of the increased need for harmony and abstraction in the face of increasing social and existential dissonance. In this respect, metaphysics could not be separated from its pathogeneses out of the malaise in the high cultures. To convince ourselves, it suffices to see how the most painful fundamental experiences of human existence are hidden beneath the fabric of fundamental metaphysical words: the One, substance, reason, God, logos, cosmos, soul, immortality, idea, order. Admittedly, they are experiences that always appear within the pure text of metaphysics as something that has already been overcome. The purpose of the pure text is to report the success of metaphysical harmonization efforts. In it, we can already hear the logical triumphs of consciousness over the dark, hurtful world.

As people of today, we can no longer easily understand the texts of such victory reports, because we have come to use different weapons from the old metaphysicians in our battles against world-weariness. But if we go back to the fundamental experiences through which metaphysics was first crystallized, we can see how metaphysics emerged as the very core of the first alternative cultures. These experiences are probably inaccessible to today's everyday consciousness at first, but they are available to contemporary conscious life at the very least when it comes to situations where treatments from modernity's pharmacy are no longer helpful. Ironically, the modern-day crisis includes involuntary access to the metaphysical attempt at world management – after all, we are watching (with a perplexity that befits primal peoples rather than late cultures) an age of a second helplessness emerge on the passive side of modernity's status as a jack of all trades. As a result, the present time, which is philosophically based on its fundamentally post-metaphysical position, has created a piquant community of experience with the old metaphysics-kindling world conditions. The threats that loomed over the world at the end of the metaphysical era reveal its beginnings as well, so much so that restorations seem inevitable. One glance at the New Age scene in North America and Central Europe gives the impression that we are dealing with a gigantic *remake*. A holistic consciousness industry has emerged on both sides of the Atlantic and it lives on metaphysical plagiarism. To put it a bit more amicably: countless contemporaries spontaneously quote from early metaphysical sources to articulate aspects of their current feelings about the world. They deem it necessary to skip over several millennia to find answers for their own questions. A portion of modernity must fall back on archaic speeches to say things for which no usable modern words exist.

What questions are we referring to? I will only discuss two here, which were essential in motivating the upsurge of thinking towards metaphysics: the inequality between different fates in life and the fear of all-devouring time. As for the first of these experiences, it was brought into language through the classical verses of the young Hugo von Hofmannsthal (one could add, with the mild somnambulist cynicism that is sometimes the privilege of poets):

> Many will of course have to die down there
> Where the heavy oars of the ships sweep
> Others reside above near the helm
> Aware of the migration of the birds and the lands of the stars.[7]

This poetic meditation aims at balancing the inequality of destinies by way of a metaphysical world-housekeeping. On that higher level which constitutes the scene of metaphysical movement, everything is both closely linked and haphazardly connected to everything else; thus, the misfortune of the one comes together with the fortune of another in a sublime harmony.

> But a shadow falls from those lives
> Across and into the others' lives,
> And the light are bound to the heavy
> As the air is bound to the earth.

Through an awareness of connection, an evident scream to the heavens becomes music to the metaphysician's ears. This desperate need for music is driven by the evidence that human destinies are unstoppably unequal and that there is no compensation for this inequality on a human level. Without a doubt, this experience points to the emergence of hierarchized large-scale societies and the separating of the fate of those at the top and those at the bottom. From there on out, the social world appears like an enchanted galley where rowing slaves perish below deck while a comprehensive view develops above in which the misery of others is redeposited into the harmony of the whole.

Many fates weave alongside my own,
All are interconnected by a common existence
And my part is more than simply this life's
Slender flame or narrow lyre.

The metaphysical impulse demands that thinking make this climb
out of the inequality and confusion of life into an order-creating
contemplation, and insofar as efforts towards order of this kind
simply belong to the very nature of thinking, we can never entirely
eliminate the metaphysical or "cosmic" holdings on the activity of
the mind – unless this activity were willing to become as incomprehensible and confused as the reality it works on, but then we
would lose the difference between mind and reality and confused de
facto existence would no longer relinquish any work to the mind.
Some mystics have indeed taken this path of indifference. But for
metaphysical thinking its task is entirely unambiguous: to show
messy life the pathways that lead to order. For us, the claim to
validity of the old metaphysical cosmic ideas of order fails because
of a simple logical distinction: an ordering contemplation is not
the contemplation of order *per se*. Music and metaphysics rise up
against the noisy physics of life as an unstoppable first alternative
because the will to order is at the very root of the entire impetus.
Metaphysical study turns away from the desolate "surface" of things
and looks down into depths or up into heights, from where intelligible order shines towards us, if we are willing to look away from
the all too visible and not see through the intrusive glow. In order
to advance to such order, the not yet refined eye and the not yet
spiritualized ear must shift to more abstract forms of hearing and
seeing – to seeing with the third eye, hearing with the third ear. This
alternative – metaphysical seeing and hearing – is always already an
overseeing and overhearing as well; a hearing all the way to the end
and a seeing through, a not listening and a looking away, a right
hearing and seeing, an inner listening and a seeing inward. The
metaphysical break with the "superficial" world of appearance grips
the organs of perception first: to ensure the effect of order, they have
to spiritualize themselves and withdraw from the gross turbulence of
what is present and existing. With that, the first step into an "enlightenment" is made – it leads to a culture of transparence where all
existing things shift from the state of being naturally lit or shaded
to that of a logical transillumination. Thus, the analytical mythos
moves into its invasive phase. The analytical mythos no longer sees
the world as a sovereign play of light and dark onto illuminated
non-luminous things; instead, it becomes the object of constant
transillumination where a permanent intellectual light pierces

through fleeting phenomena to reach eternal structures and bring them to definitive determinations. There are grounds for suspecting that the history of nihilism begins with the advent of such transillumination ontologies. If so, this history would be identical to the fate of analytical rationality which sees right through the facts to grasp their cause, through appearances to see their essence, and through structures to understand their function. This suspicion contradicts the vulgar idea of nihilism that sees the phenomenon as a modern affair and derives it from the collapse of the metaphysical "sphere." In reality, what has gone by the name of nihilism for a hundred years could only be the latest explication of the basic nihilism that has inhered in the transilluminating, backwards-leading, and, from presently tangible appearances, refraining rationalizations of the world since their emergence.

Next to the irremediable affronts on thinking by the mysteries of inequality and dissonance, the experience of death and temporality by all individual life plays a decisive role in the emergence of metaphysics. Essentially, they form one complex, and time and death are not two different experiences, but a single experience that consists of temporality. The eventual death of all individual life is already implied in the fact that everything real seems to exist "within time" and that nothing living can escape the decay that comes with the passing of time. Whatever exists in the passing of time must suffer from the illness of becoming and the injury of passing away. Whoever is born in the passage of time owes a death to nature. The Greek myth of Kronos who devours his children captures this idea in its pervasive morbidity. It speaks of life bound to time as fateful self-consumption. This idea of time has defined the Western "civilizing process" (ow!) and modernity has advanced this "fall into time" (first registered by the old metaphysics) to a consummate "chrono-latry," to quote Massimo Cacciari's baroque term for the modern cult of time.[8] But what is obscured by the contemporary dictates of clocks was glaringly obvious in the early metaphysical experience of time: Chronos,[9] the passing of time, is fundamentally a period of suffering, lack, failure – a deadline for the inevitable undoing of life.

Older metaphysical thinking was aware that the time of Chronos moves directly towards death. Metaphysics (Christian metaphysics above all) understood that, being mortals, we are zombies: the living dead, walking around in their own corpses with the ghastly pretense of being alive. Indeed, this perspective forces itself to be accepted by a thinking that has conceived of all individual life as falling prey to all-consuming time. Those who conceive of life as occurring within time and understand time as an indomitable process do not only see themselves as continuously dying but must also imagine themselves *already* as those who will have died. Together with their physical and moral being, they fall victim to Chronos – not just in retrospect, but at the outset. Life must cope with this outrage if it has understood the predicament of time in its universality. From that point on, one of the fundamental questions of conscious life is how it can cope with its irreversibility. Full of horror, the one who can imagine the passage of time with respect to their own existence will see their own flesh fall from their bones – flesh and bones that are already no longer really one's own, but that we have been dispossessed of from the outset by all-devouring Chronos. There is a reminder of this kind of shock brought on by the sight of the ephemeral in the Buddhist legend that tells of the first time that Gautama ventures outside of his father's protective palace and sees with his own eyes the suffering nature of life falling prey to time in the form of the sick person, the beggar, and the deceased. The shock penetrated so deeply that thereafter the young man no longer wished to have his "own" eyes so they could captivate him with the deadly play; he wanted to detach himself from the sense of sight and what it perceived both at the same time.

Emil Cioran is a witness to this kind of feeling in our time. In a text called *Paleontology*, he recorded the shudders of an unredeemed metaphysician when confronted with the flesh:

An unforeseen shower, one autumn day, drove me into the Museum of Natural History for a while. I was to remain there, as a matter of fact, for an hour, two hours, perhaps three. It has been months since this accidental visit and yet I am not about to forget those empty sockets that stare at you more insistently than eyes, that rummage sale of skulls, that automatic sneer on every level of zoology. ... Nowhere is one better served with respect to the past. Here the possible seems inconceivable or cracked. One gets the impression that the flesh was eclipsed on its advent, that in fact it never existed at all, that it could not have been fastened to bones so stately, so imbued with themselves ... the solidity, the seriousness of the skeleton, it seems absurdly provisional and frivolous. It flatters, it gratifies the addict of precariousness I am. That is why I am so comfortable in this museum where everything encourages the euphoria of a universe swept clean of the flesh, the jubilation of an after-life.[10]

Flesh and bones stand in ontological opposition to each other. While the flesh obscenely passes away, a promise of eternity belongs to the essence of bones. With cynical self-sufficiency, the bones perform metaphysics' rejection of this temporary life; grinning, they bode beyond flesh and transience. A gaze that looks upon the disease of life and remains unshaken can only emerge from empty eye sockets. Thus metaphysics and cynicism come into being from the same impulse; the first as an overcoming of the temporal through an ascent into timelessness and the second as a sarcastic lingering of consciousness in what is fleeting, what is null and void. Together, cynicism and metaphysics speak about this ridiculous life with the humor of destruction.

The symbol of bones shows how metaphysics' alternative to the ephemeral took shape. This alternative looks through the ominous fiction of the flesh all the way to the bony substance, to the very skeleton of life which continues to exist as a time-superior residuum. But bones only function as parables for last principles. Since they, too, are mere "apparitions," they can be reduced and converted to their nothingness. In the past, it was fire that took on the work of metaphysical alchemy, distilling the imperishable from perishable life. Whatever has gone through fire has overcome this final breakdown. What remains is imperishable essence. In the end, nothing remains from living bodies that lasts – only ash and spirit, dust and weightlessness, mineral and light. This is the substance that eternity is made of. In its last distillates, the ravenousness of time breaks down. By means of an extreme reaction, the imperishable is filtered out from the murky and volatile elements.

Thus we can see how the old metaphysics sought to cope with the irreversibly oriented-toward-death: it answered the question about an antidote to transience with eternity; its answer to the question of overcoming death was immortality. These answers were enforced as the irreversibility of life processes could no longer be compensated by older, cyclical concepts that had sufficed for a mythical interpretation of the world. Cyclical thinking only has a chance in the life forms where world-changes in linear time can be pronounced by myths of nature as never having happened. It is only in the mythic circle of nature that life is annually reborn as if nothing irrevocable, irreversible, inseparable had ever happened. However, in historical mobilized cultures, time's arrow flies irrevocably forward. In them, the irreconcilability of the fates and the transience of living conditions become overwhelmingly evident. They can only be processed with metaphysical strategies.

The metaphysical alternative (with which most of the continuances of modernity are still impregnated) contains the primordial history of human dissatisfaction with a lapsed world fallen prey to time. Radical metaphysics knew that only a radical overcoming of this reality can be its remedy. Only that which transcends life can make it bearable. And thus, metaphysics responded to the sickness of life with a witty self-cremation. Passionately, it sought the reduction of reality to its time-superior residues in matter or in spirit. It countered sickly flesh with serene bones, the burning wound with cooling stone. The metaphysical alternative has above all expressed itself consummately in the erection of stone monuments. Towering works of rock – menhirs, pyramids, temples, gates, obelisks, columns, towers – physically represent the ideals of law, permanence, and divine finality. Some of this Egypticism can still be found in the skyscrapers of New York, Chicago, and Hong Kong. In its architectures, metaphysics illustrates the thesis that the wound of time is healed only by eternal stone. In stone, the physical itself gains metaphysical content. The metaphysical exercise works ceaselessly towards a mineralization of the soul. Only those who discover within themselves the inert wisdom of the stones have found the Philosopher's Stone.

Thus, the yearning to turn to stone lends an Eleatic trait to the metaphysical need for validity. For those unable to make peace with impermanence under any circumstances, there is no greater promise of salvation than the one that lies in the discovery of the immobile. This is why God is philosophically called the unmoved mover. To become similar to him – or to restore a lost resemblance to him – the radicals of the first alternative were happy to use impossible means. Whether they went into the desert to become a grain of sand of eternity in an ecstasy of loneliness, let themselves be walled in alive to force a stand-still of the absolute with the ultimate rejection of movement or prove with crushing logic that the flying arrow stands still in the air – each time, the Eleatic effect is at play, the desire to see through false movement in order to enter into true immobility. The authentic old metaphysics abhors what moves, teems, mixes, circulates, but, above all, the revolting food cycle that requires movement and violence of the highest degree. Eat and be eaten – it is this bestial macrobiotics in particular for which metaphysical movement phobia seeks a remedy. Only a static alternative can free human existence from its movement in the direction of death. Therefore, the misery of life can be simultaneously overcome by overcoming its movement. Hardly any metaphysicians of the old kind would shy away from the thesis that only the immobile could be good whereas everything else – all greed, lack of freedom, fear, violence, misery, and exploitation – moves, whether on legs, wheels, through automation, or with motor engines.

For a few centuries now, the immobilizing affect has been exhausting itself in Europe. As a result, metaphysics of the older kind has become impossible. Since being is thought of as a verb and the subject is thought of as an activity, ontology in its classical form is no longer "tenable." Even modern science has devoted itself to a concept of movement according to its mode of operation, namely that of research; when it comes to Hegel, the suspect movement has conquered metaphysics itself and made eternity get a move on. Meanwhile, Chronos devours not only his children but also the timeless magnitudes which we once thought to have evaded his appetite. We reside in such a penetrating de-eternalization and mobilization that we are not even able to speculatively conceive of an opposite concept to the dominant concepts of movement and event. Two centuries were all it took to use up the immobilistic reserves of a world age. A cult of movement without historical precedence has enveloped modern thought and agency. It sees all that stands still, holds on, relies on itself, and rattles unused as ridiculous. As if it had to recover from a long illness, modernity has broken away from its rigidity-enamored former times and now enjoys its new power to evaporate "all that is solid." Nowadays, only real estate brokers believe in immovable property.

However, disestablished eternity casts a long shadow over the great dynamization epochs. Modernization visibly attacks the Old World basis of existence and does as much violence to the primary courses of life through increasing mobilization as the most raging immobilization. Thus, a discontent grows out of the "civilizing process" and calls forth new alternatives. Does metaphysics thereby return? Do the Egyptian and Eleatic motifs once again have a chance? Are the apostates of modernity once more seeking the exit from earthly confusion in cosmological order? Was the collapse of the old metaphysics through the attack of modern concepts of activity not definitive? Or was that first static metaphysical alternative perhaps not the only way to disagree with the world? Is there another alternative that does not have to end up in stone, purity, and self-mortification in order to cope with the transience of life?

The Second Alternative: Poeisis

It is still not broadly understood that a philosophical discourse of modernity is only possible as a critical theory of mobilization. To put this more pointedly: there is no Frankfurt school of critical theory, only a Freiburg one. Because if mobilization is indeed the basic process of modern times against which a critical theory must define itself in the form of diagnostics and therapeutics, then the Frankfurt theory has no critical principle, whether as an aesthetic theory or a theory of communicative action. As a negative aesthetic, it fails the critical moment with its latent argumentation that is without a world; as a theory of action, it becomes indistinguishable from its object insofar as communicative action manifestly operates as a principle of mobilization.[11] In contrast, the Freiburg theory has found a critical "principle" in the concept of releasement, which expresses an acute if not unmistakable difference to mobilization. The acuity of this difference consists in the fact that it describes the kinetics of modern processes as an active plunge into automatization without any illusions and then serenely recommends accepting the modern ability to act as an illness to be endured. Its ambiguousness stems from the fact that this acceptance is easily distorted into an assent to the fatal course of the world – it is but one step from intellectus fati to amor fati; one small false movement between the positivity of an understanding of the history of Being and the affirmation of calamity inherent in destiny. Nevertheless, only releasement, correctly understood, contains the difference that is able to render a theory of the world process critical – it acts not as a driving force of an alternative mobilization but as an alternative to mobilization; it does not place any other movements onto the path of the illusion that there is a path.

A critical theory of mobilization circles around the point where the kinetics of metaphysics turns into the kinetics of modernity. The old metaphysics as a passion for immobility and self-absorption is the original accumulation of subjectivity, which plunges itself forward within modernity as a passionate mobilization. Modernization takes place as the work of those powers that have catapulted out of the age of the first alternative: as the action of big science, big capital, big technology, big media. These are the essential carriers of the modern processes – and we deny ourselves an insight into their kind as long as we speak of them as "productive powers." In truth, productive powers are powers of mobilization. Mobilization is the modern response to the transience of life and the inequality of destinies. Through it, the lawsuit of dissatisfaction with the world moves to the next level of authority. The great mobilizers of modernity carry the promise of defeating the finitude and transience of the human condition by delimiting the mobilization of the finite and transitory conditions themselves.[12] The rapid planetary enforcement of this impulse illustrates the coercion with which life in post-metaphysical times seeks to cope with its irreversibility in the death-oriented process. Instead of implausible striving towards eternity, it thus brings modern dynamization strategies into play. We no longer look through smoke and mirrors at ancient images and primal sounds but have learned to banish images with images and sounds with sounds. Through the combined effect of the mobilizers, modernity forms the image of an inverted metaphysical culture. We now react to the horror of irreversible movement not with a flight into non-movement but with a flight into the fleeting. Strangely enough, modern immanentism, with its rejection of a hidden world and an after-life, has brought about no solid sense of the here and now, but has rather transformed it into a phantom and mobilized it to the point of evaporation. Heinrich Heine would revoke his most generous verses: ever since heaven has really been left to the angels and sparrows, the earth is becoming more and more unreal. A Dionysian-kinetic nihilism has superseded the metaphysical one. In it, the world is not overcome by way of the eternal, but actually revolutionized and made to disappear through the acceleration of changes. Thus, Old World metaphysics and New World technology seem to agree not to take the transient existences they encounter too seriously but to place them at the disposal of campaigns for conquest and change. In this new functional dynamism, the old Eleatic immobilism possesses its closest ally. The nihilism of transcendence is perpetuated and outbid by that of immanence. One could probably demonstrate that the newly nihilistic mobilization prevailed first and with special ferocity in those parts of the world where ancient nihilistic metaphysics and religions had tilled the ground within people's subjectivities. Seen through this optic, a nihilistic meridian becomes visible which emerged from Old Europe, from Athens, Rome, Jerusalem, Paris, and passed through Russia, Japan, and North America. Without a training to overcome the world that lasted thousands of years, there would be no modern evaporation of it. Wherever this training did not take place, modernity implants itself with great difficulty because it has no connectors to latch on to within people's mentalities. One must experience things in the world as having seen through them to their very "grounds" before developing a taste for making them dance in a kinetic revolution of modernity.

Only now does it become clear what we mean when we ask about the possibility of a second alternative. This question searches for the possibility of a non-nihilistic position of conscious life towards its irreversibility, an attitude that does not counter the death-bound passing of time with either the old nihilism of eternity and substance or the new nihilism of mobilization and change.

What we understood alternative cultures to be were remedies against the inevitable and unbearable grounds for discontent with the world – particularly against the unacceptable transience that adheres to all life which has come under the rule of an idea of time. A non-nihilistic alternative to that which is unacceptable can only stem from a different concept of time. Since the nihilistic image of the world is one that is dominated by Chronos as the passing of time, a non-nihilistic alternative must above all be one that owes nothing to Chronos. This is only possible if a present, lived time reabsorbs an imagined time. Imagined time, I argue, is the ruinous time of mortality. It stretches out between the lead up to the end and the walk backwards to the beginning – these two gestures that open up the imagined space of time's passing within a subject. But there is no reason why these gestures should compulsively and irreversibly dominate our conscious lives. The present existence is not doomed to rush forward into its imagined end, nor must it cling to the ideas of an origin, a "nature," or an initial essence. As long as it remains freely movable, it can always bring its occasional fast-forwarded imagining of the end and its momentary recourse to ideas of origin back to the balancing point in the present. Life in the moment thus stays on this side of the compulsion towards metaphysics and outside the curse of history; for neither does it have to encompass the entirety of transitory processes within historical overviews, nor does it feel it necessary to circumvent such ideas towards a concept of a non-moving eternity. The living moment is also not seduced by the suggestive idea of an infinite becoming and passing, where it would be classified as a fleeting point in time. For then, even points in temporal lines and circles would lose their character as moments in time, no longer considered to be the present.

What follows from this? Nothing less than a mildly radical critique of historical existence. If the second alternative culture actually arises from the present as its source, it will reject all of the world's structures that have been placed in the imagined space of time's passing: the mythical world of origin, the utopia of the future, the world as historical enterprise, the world as mission and mobilization.

But doesn't such presentism push aside all that counts as *interesting* about human existence? Does the retraction of imagined time back into the present not dissolve all the excitement that convinced life that it was worth living and carried it out into the adventure of history? Isn't this alternative presentism a dull, nirvana-like fundamentalism that has to ultimately fade away in an uncreative indifference?

Under the assumptions of representational thinking, these are good questions. However, if these questions do not remain inquiries but become entrenched in theses, their only use will be to illustrate the lack of understanding that this type of thinking has of the essence of presence. Whoever believes that the permanent present amounts to boredom is stubbornly imagining the present as a point in time. In truth, the present does not belong to the concepts of time. Correctly understood, it is a category of movement or drama. The present refers to the kinetic structure through which things that exist become apparent to us as that which enters the space where we encounter it. Presence is movement in the sense of the drama of arrival, emergence, and entrance. The experience of presence is one of the distinctions of human existence, because the very essence of humans is that of arrival and entry *par excellence* – we are predisposed to wake up, come out, bring forth, and begin. Presence exists only where humans do, and humans only exist where they are born. Presence is the sting of the unfinished birth.

If people live in ruinous times, they know that they are mortal – creatures for whom it befits to be drifting towards their own ruin at every moment. They have explicitly named themselves as such with melancholy correctness as long as the metaphysical era lasts. But if humans participate in presence, they are the born ones – creatures in whom the movement of birth continues. Presence as a dramatic term thus encompasses a twofold movement: the opening up of the world as arriving-from-without and the subject's holding-out of itself into the world as the space of arriving. Presence is therefore always accompanied by the awareness of a twofold happiness and a twofold horror. One instance of happiness and terror emanates from the intrusion of external powers and the arrival of unhoped-for gifts, the other from the euphoria and pain of the human exodus itself.

Because it stands in the present, the second alternative is entirely defined by natality.[13] Natal presence cannot contribute to the impulse of running ahead into one's own death; this is why it differentiates itself in its fundamental movement from the ruinous being-towards-death of the metaphysical or existentialist kind. Presence as a staying in the open arises only through the movement of human birth, and wherever this movement begins, the natal, the present, and the open attain their character in one and the same process. A life of presence realizes that something stands "before it." Metaphysics has understood the human position that implies this having of something before oneself to be mortality – which is just another way of saying that it interpreted the open "before" us as time; more precisely, as future. The modern interpretation of human existence as "historicity" is also linked to this interpretation. But the result of this historical modeling of the open-before-us is the present world with its steep increases and its reflection in our nervousness – a world that no one would dare to claim as having much time left. It is the privilege of late modern contemporaneity to know that the horizon of the world as history is no longer open. One does not necessarily have to be someone who constantly cries "Woe is me!" to grasp the end-times claustrophobia that envelops modernity's inevitable farewell to the progressive-historical filling in of the open.

But if the open before us is neither time nor future, what is it then? Now the moment has come when I have to say goodbye to my readers. As long as I have the floor to myself, it is not possible to determine what the open is on fair terms. My monologue must seem like a mock-up, blocking the subject with statements about it: what to do? Silence would not be an answer any more than the crossing out of the following sentences would – we uncomfortably recall Heidegger's clumsily significant crossing out of the word "being." In such a situation, all that remains is the retreat of assertions into asociality. From this line on, I march alone; abandoned by tradition and the public, I scribble some sentences onto the blank piece of paper in front of me that speak about the open as if it were a tangible quantity.

The question remains: if the open before us may not be presented as time or future, then what is it?

The most obvious thought is that it is simply the *space* before us that opens up before our eyes as a field of vision and action. But obviously space is also not the open *per se*, first, because space as space is filled up by its contents or elements so that we can hardly speak of an open in this case, and, second, because we must not succumb to the danger of thinking of the open as a vacuum that can be filled by the next-best thing that can seep inside to occupy it. What remains, then? If the open is not the time-before-us in the form of future and not the space-before-us in the form of a field of vision and action, then it must be understood as something that already opens up prior to the existence of spatial and temporal orientations. The reassurance of orientation is already secondary.

We notice the fact that we are "standing" in the open by feeling insecure in it. The open allows itself to be recognized by the fact that one "exists" in it. The open would then be the tension or force field that establishes itself around the eccentric human "positionality." To be in the open would therefore mean becoming aware of existential ecstasy as innate discomposure. It is in vain that our ecstatic abundance and agony always flees into space and time in order to escape its discontent with itself. The great departures and flights of humanity into historical time and geographical space, however, have led to breathtaking processes in which both become scarce – and to the certainty that if something should still be open today, it is certainly not the geographical horizon or the historical future, but the force fields of present life alone.

These force fields are the home of what modernity calls "art" and the classical tradition refers to as poeisis. Only the activities that produce something in such a way that it "stands" in the open can belong to art. The place of art as poiesis is presence – the natal force field. However, the already very old *differentiation* between art and technology reminds us that there are radical *differences* in types of production. While technology emphasizes ability and operates manufacturing as a methodically controlled making available of a product, in poiesis a trace of the natalic proceeding into presence is at work. In fact, both activities have a making character and are based on successful "art" – but they differ from the ground up in their existential content. By bringing something *forth* – that is, forward into the open – poeisis is the taking up of nature's productivity through the eccentric human subject. Its poetry continues the forth-bringing giving birth of natural life; indeed, it is poetry only to the extent that it is such a resumption and it can only be such a resumption to the extent that it succeeds at the fundamental gestures of the birth drama: coming-into-the-world and bringing-into-the-world.[14] Poiesis does what it "does right" by placing it "into presence" – not merely turning it out but bringing it *forth*, putting it out there, into the open and into the public. (Incidentally, this is where an ontopological definition of public as non-uterus emerges: that is, as a space of obstetrical "unconcealments" and as an ontological glacis of what is capable of arriving, so that it is – still incidentally – inevitable to understand public space from the concept of Heideggerian "clearing" as much as Habermasian "enlightenment.")

Through poiesis, the spirit gains maternal competencies, even if it happens to be male. This cannot be otherwise, because human productions have to follow the natural process of creation in order to follow nature as old natality into culture as new natality. However, as a new natal process, culture opens its marvelous fan and produces things that would not have occurred to old nature. It is in these risky novel productions that the human creature (stigmatized for its talent for stepping out) invents itself and its worlds. Therefore, poiesis is not a theme of aesthetics as we understand it in the modern era but one of philosophical gynecology, if I may be allowed the expression. Its jump point is the *natura naturans* that becomes cultural drama within human production and its axiom states that truth is indeed not a woman, but poiesis is a "mother." As a doctrine of bringing forth, poietology deals only with the one art in all of the arts: coming-into-the-world or *ars nascendi*, bringing into the world or *ars pariendi*, and the serene letting live or *ars vivendi*.

Needless to say, this is not the approach of the modern "civilizing process." (Now that the term has burned through the cheeks, leaving the teeth and jaws horribly visible, as with lepers, it will have to be taken out of circulation.) This "civilizing process" is expedited by technology's flight away from the open. It does not bring "forth" its products in the true sense, rather its production mode is a motherless forcing of things that function. With respect to the allocation of resources, technology is a consumption that depletes; with respect to kinetics, it is an aggressive mobilization; with respect to giving birth, it is a breeding of monsters by monsters. If that sounds harsh, then I have struck the right tone; one that is appropriate where technology leads to nothing better than the tearing apart of the great chain of life. If the question remains whether a poietic technology is possible, we would immediately speak differently about it.

The lonely stretch is now behind us and I can look for company again. It is high time that the misleading gestures used to construct this chapter were undone. They concern the order of presentation and counting of alternatives. For architectonic reasons, we had to pretend that we really believed that the second follows the first and that poiesis does not come into play until metaphysics has made its spectacular exit. Of course, that is most definitely not the case. As soon as we think of poiesis, it appears in such a way that we cannot doubt its primacy over metaphysics and technology. Because, if it is that which we claim it to be – the anthropogonic instance that dominates our ars nascendi as the art of coming-into-the-world and bringing-into-the-world – then metaphysics and technology, too, are subordinate extents in the happening of bringing forth and arriving, subordinate admittedly as problem children of natura naturans, as monster children, who not only grow to be too much for their mother but also ultimately challenge her for her reproductive competence.

The chapter did not mislead by reminding us of panic at the beginning and of poiesis at the end. Panicked culture here, poietic technology there; how is that supposed to go together? Obviously, it is not possible nor should it so long as we do not Hegelianize – that is, establish hybrid programs for calculating the incalculable. Pointing to the motif of panic brings to mind the necessity of culturally hemming in what is without measure; doing so with poiesis maps out an intensive taking of measurements of what is actually present. It is likely that we must here – post-dialectically in a demanding sense – reckon with a dual citizenship of human beings and believe them to be capable of the immense as well as the proportional, of ecstasy as well as design. There can be no synthesis of poiesis and panic in the sense of a meta-identity of measure and immeasurability. Excess and pragmatism do not result in a unified whole when put together, even if it is impossible to separate one from the other.

In the fall of 1985, I had the opportunity to visit Seoul's National Museum of Modern and Contemporary Art on a trip to Asia. In a painting by a Korean artist that was on display there, I found the paradox of contemporary reflections on time and being more lucidly visualized than in hardly any modern Western artwork. The symbol of Yin and Yang was depicted on a large canvas in light pastel shades; the venerable image of a circle made of complementary waves of light and dark, hard and soft, the eternal cipher of polarity and moving harmonization of opposites. However, in this artwork, the circle was disrupted by a flat grey wedge that split the image in two from right to left. It was as if that grey wedge wanted to refute the holistic old Asian world of roundness and completeness. It testified to a catastrophic experience of the world where the one and the other no longer add up to a "higher" unity. It was both disturbing and relieving at the same time to see how the holistic lie was here brought to an end – the split went through the image of the Tao itself. While circle and wedge do come together to create a new and more complex structure, that structure appears before us as something that is forever broken apart, injured, disjointed. Within this structure, neither could the previously harmonious circle incorporate the aggressive wedge within itself, nor was it possible for the aggressive wedge to completely alienate the two circular halves from each other and make their previous connection unrecognizable; separated, they still remind us that parts can assert their belonging to one another in a disintegrated world. Here and there, a ruined symbol also reveals the structure of something knitted, woven, consonant, netted together. Even after the destruction of the perfect roundness, old links, new links, joints and correlations remain in effect, at least as preliminary sketches of a harmonious life. From these, poiesis can form its resulting qualities. But circle and wedge do not result in a whole just as panic and poiesis do not. As soon as we grasp the common origin of both motifs to be their irreducible obstinacy, the imagined wholeness of old and new metaphysics is foiled. Of the totality of reality it is impossible to say that it is *the* whole. The paradox of wholeness ruptures all ideas of wholeness since the whole ought to be able to withstand its own disintegration and transgression but cannot. When is wholeness whole? Perhaps when it falls into nothingness as a whole.

3

EUROTAOISM?

Many will find the fact that philosophy is here transformed into a preschool of gynecology to be a severe deviation from the orthodox path. But nothing is so bad that it could not get worse – especially when we set about with heterodox energy to also gynecologize major philosophical topics like "the self," "autonomy," "freedom," "being," "nothingness." How is that supposed to work? Effortlessly: by showing in the very first section that the problem of nihilism must be addressed differently from the way Nietzsche has done it – less heroically, that is; in the second section, by developing the idea that Western metaphysics of the subject was a purely andrologically executed attempt to compensate for the uncanniness of having been born through a power-driven erection of the self, where we will not miss the opportunity to infiltrate the classical definition of philosophy as midwifery of the soul in actually gynecological terms; and in the third section, by explaining the right use of the term "Eurotaoism" – not without bringing the Old Chinese intra-uterine bonhomie into play, which interprets the carryings-on out there as a deadliness in vain.

Nothingness and Historical Consciousness: A Note on the World History of Life Fatigue

The sight of man now makes us tired – what is nihilism today if it is not *that*? ... We are tired of *man* ...
    Friedrich Nietzsche, *On the Genealogy of Morality*[1]

Nietzsche's special position in the history of newer philosophy is constituted by the fact that after him one learns to understand the connection between historical thinking and melancholy. This discovery contains the quintessential legacy of the nineteenth century. It is understandable why this century is so poorly regarded by those who came later as one of crooked postures, pompous gestures, and titanic sentimentality. Its major crime, however, is that it left the twentieth century with a paradox that seems more trying than the most hopeless double bind. By bringing up those who are born later to think historically, it infected them with an incurable melancholy. Its historicism destroyed the immune system of naïve life that protects it from seeing itself historically and provided it with a vision of its forlornness in the great realms of time. Just as Pascal shuddered before the eternal silence of infinite space, so the humans of historicism must have felt dejected when faced with the eternal noise of historical epochs. History's lesson for the present time is that it gives us reasons to despair of it. For this reason, historicity is the philosophical code word for depressiveness – we have known this ever since the young Nietzsche insightfully pointed to the disadvantage of history for life. One can assume that the generation of romanticists who consisted of witnesses and survivors of the French Revolution already had to suffer through the detrimental side of historical mobilization; for them, the evil of the century lay in the feeling that this historical world was nothing but a graveyard of enthusiasms – all the beautifully begun projects rot within it. Since then, thinking historically means orienting oneself in a situation where life is no longer a match for its own reflectivity. This, too, has been the subject of the European philosophy of alienation since the work of Hegel's students. Their critique revolves around a structure where life discovers that it is equipped with more morality than vitality, more memory than enterprising spirit, more inhibitions than drives. Only historicism makes palpable the nightmare of the past generations that burdens present ones. Aside from a small amount of scholarly happiness, there is hardly a thought within this structure that is not marked by anger at the outcome of history. We constantly succumb to it as into an enormous inhibitory device that imposes itself on us in the form of civilization, education, memory, conscience, lesson plan, capital, objective spirit. In historicism, every life has the feeling of having arrived too late. It finds itself in the position of an heir who realizes only after the fact that the inheritance that was to make them rich is actually overcharging them and leading them into ruin. Among rebellious spirits, this discovery translates into the furious flight forward.[2]

The effect of being ruined by an unprovable and inviolable inheritance is extraordinarily ironic. We must remember that European historicism first began as an optimistic enterprise of appropriating humanity's entire past as our prehistory. The heroic optimism of total historical appropriation is primarily linked to the works of Hegel and Marx: Hegel attempted to reclaim the total past of all thinking humans as the property of a self-resonating absolute spirit, while Marx asserted the claim of organizing the entire future as an expression of the essence of a humanity that wades through itself to get to itself. For a long time now, however, the impression has been spreading that these two greatest programs known to recent history both lead to exhaustion in their respective ways. We are just happy if nothing happens to us on our way to work and we cannot even imagine hoping to convert the world into a condominium for our species via our work. To this day, the earth is regarded by ideologues in the succession of Marx as a future single-family house of the working class, while for Hegel, world history is a family tomb in which each skull represents a relative. Both of these massive endeavors fall back into the universal history of fatigue, and in view of both of these last two great Titanisms, it becomes increasingly clear that the more historicity reflects on itself, the more it comes under the sign of Saturn. As far as depressive historicism is concerned, the present is characterized only by the fact that it perceives fatigue not only retroactively, but also prospectively. Today, you do not have to be a historian so much as a futurologist to have history come to mind as a patchwork of despair. Nowadays, those who feel like being sad think not so much about what once was but about what the already surprisingly recognizable future will bring. Now that historicism has usurped the future as well, the circle of historicity is closed. World history in the form of an energetic account made on the steps that lead up towards us is no longer easily possible and will heretofore always be sabotaged by counternarratives that speak of losses and fractures. Thanks to historical enlightenment, the world is now under the eye of a sad science – unable to be romanticized; the best remembrance has the most evil eye. As a result, all history is dis-evangelist – history is bad news.

At this point, the question of nihilism can be introduced. It is obvious that in the declarations of nihilism as they arose barely more than a hundred years ago, the affirmability of life as a whole was called into question. This is directly related to the triumph of historicism and its disenchantment with the temporal world. It creates a cultural situation where life has to see its own history as a process of increasing inhibitions and deformities. Historicism, as an application of enlightenment onto the existence of the enlighteners themselves, dismantles reasons to live and dissolves the vigorous self-invention of local narcissisms in a relativistic way. Therefore, the issue of nihilism must become the focal point of modern cultural self-understanding at a time when the victory of inhibitions over impulses, depression over initiatives, comparison of lifestyles over the decision to choose one is almost complete. This is precisely Nietzsche's moment. He positions his thinking at the lowest point of universal historical decadence on the assumption of having reached a turning point at the same time. He understood that historicism and nihilism are allies insofar as a historical reflection that is thought through to its inevitable end can be about nothing other than the history of an unstoppable nihilistic inhibition of life which enforces itself out of Europe onto the entire world in the name of high religion, morality, and civilization.

For Nietzsche, the history of the Christian West unfolds as that of a slow-moving suicide. In it, life-denying impulses permeate all forms of thought, sensations, arts, and institutions with fearsome thoroughness. The psychological term for this process is the seizure of the power of resentment; the biological term, decadence; the religious term, Christianity; the philosophical term, nihilism. For Nietzsche, the world history of Christian resentment is the story of an immeasurably consequential devaluation of life and world. This devaluation is the aggressive spike in negation that emerges from the feelings of resentment of an already denied, inhibited, mutilated life. In the Christian rejection of the world, a whiff blows over to us of the suicidal depths of Asia. For Nietzsche, Western nihilism is the world history-making enactment of a radical negation of all that he calls the vital "values"; in it, he sees a will to nothingness at work that empowers negative stirrings instead of vital self-affirmations. What our nihilism wants would be nothingness as the highest value. This is a nothingness in the form of an absence of valuing life as worthwhile, an absence of the motivation to exist; in short, a depressed nothingness rooted in the refusal to accept life as it is. The exploration of motivational nihilism runs through Nietzsche's entire body of work. With angry lucidity, he works out the mechanisms of the inhibited and inhibiting negation that has acquired a theoretical, moral, and psychological monopoly in the modern age. Disguised as Christian mission, philanthropy, and civilizational progress, Western nihilism has gained the power to move the world and bring it down at the same time. Talk of nihilism forced itself upon the waking spirits of the nineteenth century because they understood how powerlessness had established itself as a world power. The inability to reach a comprehending affirmation of life gained favor in institutions that constitute a disguised denial of life. Nihilistic modernity is the world realm of resentment in the form of a will to break life. With this diagnosis, Nietzsche has issued the moral death certificate to the West and its heirs in the East and West.

With outrage, he reminded us that the word "world" is a Christian expletive. Seeing the world be dominated by the Christian "no" that was masked itself as post-Christianity, he felt justified in taking the side of denied life and disdaining his age as an era of consummate nihilism. Instead, he taught a Dionysian law of nature – the right of life to follow motivations other than moral ones. His utopia was a heroic positivism by way of which a positive, noble self-affirmation without consequences could dissociate itself from any origin that consisted of poisoned emotions.

All this is well known and only sketched out here as a background for what comes later. Of course, no one will deny the combat value of Nietzsche's diagnoses, nor cast doubt on the strategic reach of his religion-critical gaze. Nevertheless, in order to talk about the dynamics of nothingness today, we can no longer continue directly in the tradition of Nietzsche's theorems. Strange as it sounds, his conception of nihilism remains philosophically too innocuous, to the extent that it stops at motivational nothingness and its "overcoming."

"We are tired of man ..." – this sentence, more than its author knew, succumbs to a process where the increasing effort of human existence triggers a wave of life fatigue. This process also includes Nietzsche's escape from fatigue into violent affirmations and walks right past the Dionysian revivals as if bored by them. After its misleading upswings, thinking has to come to the decision to perceive its own gravity, fatigue, and vested depression in positive terms. We will show that a meditation on gravity is needed to enliven philosophical talk about nothingness and nihilism. Nietzsche's genealogy of morality and his analysis of the feelings of resentment are not enough to understand gravity. At best, they elucidate the will to nothingness but they fail before the (perhaps more sophisticated?) task of locating nothingness in a prehistory of negation and in an archeology of life fatigue. Depression as an existential experience of gravity is in the last instance not a psychiatric issue but a philo-sophical one.

Nietzsche himself has occasionally looked beyond the horizon of motivational nihilism. His gaze went furthest in the famous formu-lation that describes modern nihilism as an uncanny guest – the most uncanny of all guests. The metaphor of the guest points to the idea that nothingness is more than just a product or goal of the denial of life by those who live poorly. It suggests that conscious life must, in principle, be prepared for terrible visitors. Human existence itself has an uncanniness to it that does not only then emerge when humans say no to the given. More powerful and older than any yes or no we speak, the uncanny is already present in the medium of that yes or no. The eerie guest who haunts the moderns is a descendant of the uncanny where we are always already a guest owing to the sheer fact that we exist. Thus, nothingness is not so much the guest as it is the host. However, Nietzsche was of the opinion that the uncanny comes to us rather than vice versa, and thus lapsed into the heroic key. He led us to believe that "living dangerously" was an ethos of the more noble self and not a common situation that precedes every effort and achievement.

With the reference to the uncanny, a new – say anthropological or fundamental ontological – tone enters into the discussion of nothingness. Now, talk is no longer of motivations and valuations but of the structure of existence into which the imprints of the negative are engraved. At the height of the recent philosophical discussion about existence, it could even have been said that it ended up in nothingness; in other words, in the ungiven and the ungrounded. Such formulations demonstrate the movement that entered the analytics of nothingness during the twentieth century. At the same time, nothingness has made itself an ontologically popular career and has risen to stardom in novels, films, and children's books. Just how far one can go in this direction is shown by Michael Ende's fantasy cult fairy tale *The Neverending Story*, where nothingness turns into something that grows in massiveness by absorbing the most tangible realities. Of course, the book will be accused of translating metaphysics and myth into kitsch, but the level of popularization of metaphysical ideas that it reaches is itself a fact of intellectual history that deserves attention. With Ende, nothingness achieves a concreteness that would make a sworn Heideggerian blanch. For those on whom the book has not made an indelible impression, we will remind them of the passage where the young hero Atreyu encounters three forest spirits on his exodus – strange bark trolls who warn him to continue on his way, for if he were to take the path straight ahead, he would walk directly into nothingness:

A cold shiver ran down his spine at the sight of them. The first, having no legs or haunches, was obliged to walk on his hands. The second had a hole in his chest, so big you could see through it. The third hopped on his right foot, because the whole left half of him was missing, as if he had been cut through the middle.[3]

The three characters who are gnawed at by nothingness play a role that myth research refers to as that of the adjuvant, the helper who first appears in a warning function and then to show the way. As Atreyu asks what happened to them, the first answers:

"The Nothing is spreading.... It's growing and growing, there's more of it every day, if it's possible to speak of more nothing. All the others fled from Howling Forest in time, but we didn't want to leave our home. The Nothing caught us in our sleep and this is what it did to us."
"Is it very painful?" Atreyu asked.
"No," said the second bark troll, the one with the hole in his chest. "You don't feel a thing. There's just something missing. And once it gets hold of you, something more is missing every day. Soon there won't be anything left of us."[4]

Then Atreyu asks – curious, as all saviors are – where in the forest it had begun, and after hearing the trolls' answer, he climbs a tall tree to look at the nothingness:

When at last he reached the crown, he turned toward the sunrise. And then he saw it: The tops of the trees nearest him were still green, but the leaves of those farther away seemed to have lost all color; they were gray. A little farther on, the foliage seemed to become strangely transparent, misty, or, better still, unreal. And farther still there was nothing, absolutely nothing. Not a bare stretch, not darkness, not some lighter color; no, it was something the eyes could not bear, something that made you feel you had gone blind. For no eye can bear the sight of utter nothingness. Atreyu held his hand before his face and nearly fell off his branch. He clung tight for a moment, then climbed down as fast as he could. He had seen enough. At last he really understood the horror that was spreading through Fantastica.[5]

Rarely does one find such a complete description of "actually present" nothingness. It is only through such a description that we truly see how talk of nothingness has spread within new-metaphysical phantasms as a code word for the horrifying. It gnaws on the characters like an ontological leprosy, turning trees transparent like a metaphysical forest extinction. It is as if the illuminating light operated as a secret agent of nothingness and, as in negative theology – it can ultimately only be spoken of in negations – always in such a way that it is determined by its unbearableness to the human eye. Taken together with the hint that this nothingness raids the forest from "sunrise" on, this brings to the fore the idea that the triumphant march of nothingness could be related to the development of a certain Western metaphysics of light. Ende's portrait of nothingness is thus not entirely without resemblance to the original, and some claim it to have poetic charm. Despite this, it plunges the poor creatures whose job it is to do philosophy into a spirited dilemma. They don't know whether to pull their hair out from envy at such vividness, or whether they should throw the book into the corner out of anger at such raw concretism. This dilemma can only be brought to an end by discovering another form of visual clarity that takes up the concept with the charms of a children's book but without assuming a regression in thinking. Is it possible to speak of nothingness in an engaging way without depicting it as a discoloring agent and omnivorous animal?

So let us follow the tracks of nothingness with philosophical means. On our way to a different kind of vividness, we begin to tell of the movements of the children of men that go from the lawful to the appalling and from the domestic into the uncanny. One more step, and we write the opening chapter of a philosophical novel that tells of human birth and the further adventures of the subject. It would not be a philosophical novel if it did not try to claim to be a general autobiography in which all that says "I" has recorded its story. This novel of the subject has a Pantagruelian mix of genres. It combines equal parts of the history of philosophy as well as the ghost story, the heroic epic as well the Picaresque novel, and must also include something of hagiography. It is the novel of birth, written as the prototype for all stories that tell of the excursion, odyssey, heroic path, and education in the labyrinth of the world. We will see how a coming into the world and coming to naught echo each other. As a by-product of this natural history of the uncanny, a summary social history of human over-exertion and a small world history of life fatigue emerges. It is a book of the human being as a questionable child of the world – not a book for children.

The Miscarried Animal and the Self-Birth of the Subject

Man is the great —— in the book of nature.
Jean Paul, "Selections from the Papers to the Devil"[6]

If we follow the footsteps of the uncanny all the way back to the origin, we encounter the human drama of birth. The way that humans come into the world presumably contains the complete key to the code of the problem of nothingness. If the word "nothing" is supposedly more than a pretext for charlatanism, then it is the indication that for humans it does not suffice to be born in order to arrive in the world: the physical birth of a human is the opposite of a coming-into-the-world; it is the dropping out from all that is "familiar," a plunge into the uncanny, finding yourself exposed in a frightening location. This is true in three ways. First, for the human child, being born means bidding farewell to its intra-uterine life, which is probably the only stage of its reception in the world that has a truly hidden, homey character – provided that the foothills of the predatory outside world do not encroach on it; in any case, the birth exodus into the world is an adventure ride through uncanny forests that render the spookiness of Atreyu's forest[7] rather bourgeois by comparison. Second, coming into the world means arriving in uncertainty – because for humans more than any other beings, the world is something that does not get defined from the outset, that is not a foregone conclusion, but something that has to be determined and established. The place of arrival itself is made uncertain and set in motion by the arrival of the human, that constructive animal; anyone who had the bad idea to fall out of the womb straight into Tokyo, Mexico City, New York, or Cairo will soon have a song to sing about the uncanny life in the thicket of cities. And, third, for humans, giving birth always means getting there way too early and finding oneself in a state that is absolutely unsuitable for a successful arrival in reality, a state of total disorientation, helplessness, and embarrassment. The only thing that helps us in this exposed situation is the fact that in the beginning, the world to which we come is identical, with one small exception, to the mother from whom we come. This small exception is precisely the measure of ontological difference. Because as soon as we are old enough to get to know our mother from the outside, we begin to get to know a "world" that is not our mother. It may be said that the strange difference between mother and non-mother preoccupies humans for the rest of their lives, because they can never quite understand how the world that at first felt like the mother could transform into the world that looks the way we know it to look now – we will not say how, to avoid summoning panic into the room.

If we want to start from a reflected concept of the world, we can no longer seriously claim that humans come into the world via their birth. A nameless something is put in a position of which it cannot promise itself anything certain or good unless it had arrived to a mother and people who promise it a certain and good world. This has a far-reaching consequence for the philosophical concept of the world: the world in which the human newcomer arrives is, by its very nature, nothing more than a promise that the older inhabitants of the world make to the newcomers, a promise predestined to be broken owing to the liability of worldly conditions. With this, the question of nothingness takes on a new form. Nothingness can now either mean that nothing is promised to those who come into the world, so that they cannot promise themselves much from their own human existence either, and consequently develop an inclination to return from whence they came, into the womb, to death, into the monist all-nothingness – a motif that has its place in all redemptive religions and all doctrines of all-in-one unity. Or it suggests that nothing will come of the great promises that were made and that none of the expectations of the world that have been roused in us by mothers will be fulfilled in a world as non-mother – a motif that all versions of worldly-wise skepticisms, cynicisms, and nihilisms deal with. The uncanniness of the human coming into the world therefore has its grounds in the unreliability of human promises. Does this stem from individual recklessness, from irresponsibility, from the moods of the unpredictable bipeds? No – it stems from the fact that the world given as a promise has something untenable in itself, or, if tenable, then only with luck and effort. In the uncanny, the unstoppable tendency of promises appeals to us to the point of untenability. That is why our coming-into-the-world has a pull into nothingness from the outset. Even though every birth is also inherently a promise to the world, in every promising birth a succumbing to the untenable is also at play because the promised world is marked by untenability. It even has to be said that a hint of miscarriage adheres to every birth. Humans do not arrive as solid subjects into robust worlds; rather the world emerges for them through the fact that they are born slightly to the side and exposed to the ungiven, the uncanny. Nietzsche only half-formulated this relationship when he spoke of nihilism as the uncanny visitor who haunts modern existence. It is not that an otherwise saddle-proof life receives terrible visits in rare crises – it is already a visit into the uncanny of its own accord. We always run off course, we always drift a little bit further away; in the great chain of being, humans are an open link.

As a living being, the human is therefore a pure problem, a chronic miscarriage. From the outset, there is a gap between each newly born individual and previous life up to that point – this gap opens up each time insofar as the forced displacement that the newly born endure at their arrival reaches into the uncanny. This gap is the space where we experience nothingness as something that can be "present" and into which we have been placed. The world is built into this gap; earth can rise and arrive in it; the ropes of promises stretch across it as people venture out onto them like tightrope walkers.

In the shadow of these considerations, it becomes apparent that the human is not simply a "living being" endowed with reason, but a being who must "lead" their life. Without a way of life, human life is nothing in the double sense, neither life nor human. But people have to promise their lives to themselves before they can lead them. As for us, the decisive thing is done under the guidance of life-giving promises, and thus we depend on them from our first to our last day. Without the inflow of affirmations that promise and validate our lives, we cannot keep ourselves alive psychologically or biologically – according to paleoanthropological findings, people who are cut off from all promises die a psychogenic death within forty-eight hours. The human standard of living is always disputed by promises. If human beings are not living beings, but life-leading beings, then the source of a specifically human fragility is here laid bare: the leading of their lives depends on the keeping of promises that tend towards the untenable of their own accord. When mothers take their crying children into their arms and assure them that *everything will be ok*, they promise them more than can be kept – but they also cannot not promise it to them if they do not wish to let their children sink prematurely into untenability. Each individual learns early enough that the hard shadow of untenable promises falls upon human life and that existence entails not only standards of living and leading a life on the basis of kept promises, but also substandard living and the misleading of life because of promises not kept.

These circumstances help explain why life comes to account for its primary uncanniness only involuntarily and under the utmost duress. It is, after all, the usual point of "accounting" to present life as something predictable, meaningful, familiar, and reliable. The primordial promise of life, philosophically called reason, is to object to the failure to keep promises and to insist that reason delivers what it promises – was reason not at one time also an expression for the influx of auspicious reasons to live for our already ever-endangered existence? That is why reason has the structure of a self-sustaining promise for us, and the invasion of the unreasonable is generally perceived as scandalous and devastating because when the promise of reason is broken, it may seem that there is ultimately nothing to the promises of the world and of life.

These considerations make it clear why an anthropology that has not worked its way through a theory of birth must remain insipid: only philosophy of birth can become so attentive to the abyssal side of human coming-into-the-world that it fuses the term "world" together with the drama of arriving in it. From a birth-philosophical point of view, the human is the being who had the power not to be an animal and to venture out into a world that is only "given" by promise. In this respect, anthropology is nothing more than the science of recklessness – of human beings' frivolity in establishing ways of life upon promises. Who could deny that the

Book of History contains a great variety of impostures generated by promises? And who can escape the impression that the people of the highly cultural, that is, promising era have promised themselves something that will probably not be possible to be kept in the long run; that the psychologico-cultural and technical apparatuses that were built to keep the wrong promises are themselves approaching collapse by now in order to keep up with the untenability of what was promised?

Anthropology as a science of such recklessness becomes the central discipline of philosophy as soon as it elaborates a general concept of the subject as a holder of untenable positions. What the subject and what subjectivity is can therefore no longer be adequately grasped with conventional philosophical formulas – it is neither a substrate in the sense of the Greek Hypokeimenon, nor a pure acting or bringing forth in the sense of the modern philosophies of activity, but an ensemble of behaviors that can be grouped around the basic gestures of carrying, making, and keeping. If the world already has the form of a promise for humans in its given condition, then the human being is – insofar as it is "in" the world and has "come" to it – as the subject and receiver of the promise also already its carrier and keeper. Even the famous "self-preservation," which has been philosophically often determined as the foundational aspiration of subjectivity, is in turn a descendant of that holding by which the world is kept and carried on as a promise through subjective efforts. The fact that modern philosophy has placed its principle in active subjectivity of course already suggests that it has found the courage to embark on a history-making adventure in order to promise itself the utmost from its own actions in the world. What else is the philosophy of subjectivity other than a logical machine that believes it has identified the keeper of all possible promises in the free-thinking and -acting subject? As free-thinking and acting, the human is regarded from the ground up as the self-preserving, auspicious being. As subject, the human is the guarantor of the promises with which the miscarried animal gives itself its world. Only where the subject renders its stabilizing contribution does the world get held up as "given" for human beings. By means of this contribution alone, the arrival of newborns does not immediately lead to a fall into bottomlessness. The subject as self-keeper of the promises given to it delays its fall at a tolerable stage. This delay or holding up is the effort-that-I-am. Subjectivity as an act of self-preservation is therefore not a calm substrate but a self-exertion. It is no coincidence that the philosophies of subjectivity at their highest level lead to theories of work – after all, the term "work" (even after its deceptive career at the firm of Hegel and Marx) still preserves a memory of the archaic efforts to keep the promises of the world, and if we know today that the equation of subject and "worker" is based on a productivist short-circuit, there are still good reasons to point out their relationship of origin in terms of subjectivity and exertion.

Funnily enough, the philosophies of the subject have made a lot of fuss about the subject's spontaneity – people wanted to sniff out the tracks of freedom within it. In truth, the philosophy of the subject is not so much interested in freedom as in the priming of possible outlets for the effort-that-I-am. What is called spontaneity is basically the self-imposed exertion towards effort, which drifts and ferments in the subject as kinetic energy. It is hardly surprising that the freedom-impassioned philosophies of the subject could not uncover the reason for exertion in the subject itself. In all of the talk of activity, spontaneity, obligation, and desire together with the source metaphorical indulgence in the "arising from within oneself," it was misunderstood that the basic exertion or effort that flows into spontaneity stems from a trace of miscarriage on the human. The human becomes subject only because of and to the extent that it does not come into the world only by leaving its mother's womb, but has to offer up enormous additional efforts to establish and maintain the world into which it comes. Although subjectivity is, as idealism has taught us, only understandable from the omen of pure activity, this in turn is not a "deed," neither a Fichtean self-positing nor Sartre's self-choosing, but rather one with the already exerted effort in contrast to the pre-subjective abandonment into the uncanny, to bring oneself by means of self-birth into the world and gain status in it through one's own self-stance. A subject is everything that tries to become and be its own world for itself – how? By sticking to itself, its "principles" and its concern for itself. This self-stance has several faces: it appears as abstinence, as a holding oneself to chosen norms, as self-reliance, as self-preservation, as self-justification.

Therefore it is not surprising that the history of the subject has been a history of *stances* since the very beginning. From the Stoics to existentialism, from the glowing desert saints to the cool young city dwellers, the subject always steps in front of us as a self-composed center of effort, as the active principle of an exerted stance against the sluggish, shapeless, and depressing outside world. Whether the subject holds itself up as an ascetic self by abstaining from all seductive, disruptive, and frightening influences; whether it stands up to the hopeless and untenable world by holding on to the belief in God or godliness; whether it constitutes itself as an autonomous self, sustained by a philosophizing reason, which is, in turn, appointed as the self-guardian of its laws; whether it tries to maintain itself as a conqueror of life fatigue in order to make itself heroically and self-extravagantly a gift to the world; whether it knows itself, gloomily resigned to self-acceptance, to be held out into nothingness; whether it rides the waves on the surfboard of its desire in anti-oedipal exhilaration; whether it angrily sticks to the style of its terribly splintered way of writing before sovereignty, and watches from the corners of its eyes as it eludes itself: the subject is always there to give itself a firm foothold in a stance through efforts that resemble a self-birth. Through its inevitably monstrous position, the subject is "spontaneously" condemned to the effort to stabilize its hold by means of its own promises in a world taken over on revocation.

According to their purpose, stances are always expectations of the world's continued existence and of the keeping of its promises – not least also expectations of the repeatability of once acquired programs. Even those who are committed to the Stoic doctrine of *nil admirari* and no longer promise themselves anything from the world at least expect that the world will no longer agitate them out of their stance through some kind of a surprise. Then the house of cards of external conditions may by all means collapse as long as one's stance musters the power to persevere, as long as the subject's status remains unaffected by the upheavals of external holdings. As self-holder and self-carrier, the subject cannot help but become set on tendentially world-less or at least counter-worldly attitudes – after all, it lives, as we have seen, only on the effort to bring itself forth and outward through a self-birth like the keeping of its own promises or those it has appropriated. Thus, the self-sustaining activity of the subject is inseparable from a certain counter-worldly self-breeding – Foucault would say self-care – which serves a heightened coming-into-the-world.

Nietzsche is more responsible for this than other, newer thinkers. It was he who, in his *Genealogy of Morality*, elevated the subject's autogenesis to a philosophical agenda.

> To breed an animal with the prerogative to *promise* – is that not precisely the paradoxical task which nature has set herself with regard to humankind? is it not the real problem *of* humankind?
> ... That is precisely what constitutes the long history of the origins of *responsibility*. That particular task of breeding an animal with the prerogative to promise includes ... the ... task of ... *making* man ... predictable. Let us place ourselves ... at the end of this immense process where ... we then find the *sovereign individual* ... a man with his own, independent,

enduring will, whose *prerogative it is to promise* ... the possessor
of an enduring, unbreakable will.[8]

How does nature come to take on such a demanding task with
regard to humans? How does it lapse into the idea of creating beings
who have to plunge into the adventure of self-generation so that
they can live? Nietzsche leaves these questions unanswered – but
his way of speaking of nature's self-posed task invites us to think
of an ambitious mother who celebrates herself in her children. In
Nietzsche's rhetoric of increase and breeding, the self-generating
process of increased life in the wake of highest promises comes
very clearly to prominence. The clear text version of this idea can
be found – one would like to say: of course – in Karl Marx, who
in Nietzsche's year of birth in 1844 identified man as a born self-
generator: "Because socialist man understands the whole of what is
called world history as nothing but man's creation through human
labor ... he has the observable, irrefutable proof of his birth through
himself."[9] Of the triumphs and torments of self-generating effort,
however, it is only Nietzsche, not Marx, who can convey a term
because he, unlike the thinker of socialism, knows that in the self-
birthing of the self, it is not "work" that is at stake, but burdens of
pregnancy, birth pains, suffering, labors in the English language, the
struggle for existence, *ponos* in the Greek language, the inevitable
self-generating expropriations of life to which no reappropriation
corresponds, and at best the euphoria of taking a deep breath
outside.

> What do I find absolutely intolerable? Something which I just
> cannot cope alone with and which suffocates me and makes me
> feel faint? ... That something failed comes near me. ... Apart
> from that, what cannot be borne in the way of need, depri-
> vation, bad weather, disease, toil, solitude? Basically we can
> cope with everything else, born as we are to an underground
> and battling existence; again and again we keep coming up
> to the light, again and again we experience our golden hour
> of victory, – and then there we stand, the way we were born,
> unbreakable, tense, ready for new, more difficult and distant
> things.[10]

The subject's self-birth, Nietzsche's formulas say, is a birth into
standing. Marx also provides the consonant second voice: "A being
only counts itself as independent when it stands on its own two
feet and it stands on its own two feet as long as it owes its existence
to itself."[11] Thus, this type of birth leads directly into the vertical,

that is, to standing thanks to one's own erection, without sidelong glances for possibilities of tolerably lying down or fundamentally being carried. Because it is about immediate self-establishment, the self-born and increasing subject for Nietzsche is also not the same as the passively born, misguided subjects who – because they themselves are reduced, poisoned, suffocated – can't help but spread an atmosphere of asphyxiation and reduction around them, much to the agony of those who still carry the sting of success in their flesh. That is why the determined self-birthers must repel the obscenely comfortable, mediocre, and atrophied.

> … but who would not, a hundred times over, prefer to fear if he can admire at the same time, rather than not fear, but thereby permanently retain the disgusting spectacle of the failed, the stunted, the wasted away and the poisoned?[12]

The willingness to face what is frightening is given to the self-birther as a sign of election, that is, as a spur of self-intensification. The intensity of the subject is synonymous with the urge of its being pregnant with itself. What the subject can bring forth from itself through the force of its exertion is always only itself, and the world, into which it will come, can never be any other than its own, self-designed, self-generated. By energetically bringing itself to its own world, the subject opens up an unbridgeable distance to the world of others. From this distance – maintained by the self-care of the self-producing subject – the abstinent stances arise for which the Greeks coined the word "askesis," and the moderns the term "individuality." If the self-emphasizing subject displays a brittle stance towards foreign-worldly seductions – talk, fame, topicality, women, princes, careers – it is not from morbid or self-torturous inclinations (as befits a corrupt notion of asceticism), but out of the clear instinct of wanting to serve only a single effort.

> His "motherly" instinct, that secret love towards what is growing inside him, shows him places where he can be relieved of the necessity of thinking about himself … *not* … out of virtue, out of a creditable will to moderation and simplicity, but because their supreme master *so* demands … it is [his] dominating instinct, at least during periods when they are pregnant with something great.[13]

What Nietzsche discovers here is the birth of asceticism from the requirements of self-birth. Asceticism in the fundamental sense does not reject the will; it is, on the contrary, an expression of a strong pooling of will, an energetic summary of all partial drives in a single ray of will. Nietzsche's discourse on the will to power is also latently at the service of this thought and remains incomprehensible without this discovery. In it, the idea of the possibility of a univocal existence of language inches forward – it is the idea of the possibility of a monothematic will. Only the monothematics of the will steers the will towards itself and thus onto the self-bearing track. All that an ultimately pooled-together will to oneself can possibly want is *eo ipso* self-making, self-reliance, self-birth, self-realization. To the extent that asceticism is an exercise of the will to abstain from parasitic auxiliary drives and stray impulses, it serves the self-bearing erection of the subject.[14] Through it, it becomes its own content – because only those who know to abstain can contain themselves, find themselves to be enough, keep themselves upright, and become those who stand, hold, carry, set up, give, and found from their "own efforts."

In this program of a self-upright-holding stance, it is impossible not to hear the masculinist tenor. The suspicion arises that the subject of the philosophers is perhaps nothing more than a logically encoded fantasy about the possibility of permanent erection from cradle to grave. In the self-born formation of the subject, the dynamics of masculinity as an urge to one's own standing are actually at work. Masculinity in the narrowest sense of the word exists only in connection with the history-making illusion of the independent erection – the philosophical code word for this is subject autonomy. Since the days of Plato, the phenomena of vocation to self-birth, male high-feeling, and existential self-intensification in thought have been intimately interwoven; an impetus of Eros into the vertical pulses through all of them. Can it be a coincidence that in Socrates the metaphysics got under way as Maieutic, that is, as an obstetrics for a subjectivity that has to fight its way out of the womb-grave of the body in order to keep itself upright in the heights of ideas? This peculiarly masculine obstetrics has created a historical precedent. What has been promoted to the light of the world by the art of philosophical midwifery in Greek antiquity has consequently continued to develop the metaphysics of work and technology as a mechanical uterus of human self-fabrication over the course of more than two thousand years. The Maieutic of the subject, metaphysics, and technology are each only aspects of the same phenomenon, which, with its grandeur as with its riskiness, has the historical world holding its breath: aspects of the self-birth of the man-human. This takes place as a conquest of the vertical, as a revolution of self-born sovereignty against the humiliation of the old way of birthing, thus as a repulsion against old nature and as the establishment of a phallic will of its own against the dictatorship of mothers. Through a colossal tearing away of oneself, the andrological subject has begun to be self-interested and has mobilized as the commissioner of its own worlds. But it is precisely through its mobilization that it is finally confronted with the questions of how, after all, it intends to deal with nature as its origin, and whether it really believes it will escape its first birth via its second.

Among those who have let this question be asked, Martin Heidegger stands out in a twilight greatness with his attempt at a new thinking of being. This is to be understood quite literally – because what constitutes Heidegger's meaning is inseparable from the threefold problem that is incarnated in him; the problem of preeminence, of greatness, and of twilight.

Heidegger looms – to engage with his thought, we have to begin from this perception. Because for most, dealing with what looms is annoying or overwhelming; there is usually no engaging, but either aversions or subjugations. But when dealing with Heidegger, it is a question of recognizing in the looming itself the problem to which his thinking bears witness. In fact it is like this: Heidegger not only looms "forth," he is also the thinker of looming, of standing out, of erecting oneself, of bringing forward. By emphasizing within the event of truth its moments of unconcealment, emergence, opening, and clearing, he grasps – like no metaphysician before him – the kinetics of being as a coming forward, a placing into the open, and a being challenged to the open expression of presence-ing.[15] It is fair to say without exaggeration that Heidegger, instructed by his own outstanding dynamism, was the only thinker of the philosophical tradition able to conceptualize what *placing* means according to its onto-kinetic nature. For him, it is the visible (and, through excessive visibility, equally hidden) gesture of the "occurrences of being" – insofar as the equation of being and being brought forth is valid. The taste of being, as he notes, adheres only to what is capable of "existing," which also takes part in the ecstasy of being brought forth. Being is the ontological aroma of that which is in front, up high, and spoken out loud. To attain it, entities must have been brought forward natally, brought upward phallically, and evocatively come up for discussion. Only in an austere decision-making climate, where nothing lies around or stands there undecided, but everything is taken up decisively, does human existence know itself as "great." By letting itself be challenged, it accepts its emergence into the arena of being, and by assuming only important things as a challenger, it rises up to the level of that by which it has been "enframed."[16] It is great through standing up to the enormous; greatness becomes its aura by the fact that the having-been-placed-upright has nothing to do with anything less than with the "fate of being" itself. Heidegger's looming corresponds to the self-consciousness of a being-there that sees itself as the location of a Titans' battle for being. Its atmosphere of greatness is the shiver of the air over the ontological battlefield. There is something of a metaphysical priapism in it – painfully heaved up towards the most important thing, it rises up with a heroic positioning into the bald skies of being and nothingness. In these erections, however, it is true that the subject, who has been necessarily forced to greatness, does not stand upright of its own accord. Heidegger knows that the grammar of placing upright is imbued with an irony: precisely that which stands itself upright is the most upright-placed. The new thinking of being can subvert subjectivity and its game of placing because – in a more or less explicit way – it sees all self-births from the point of view of the first birth, understands all phallic installations from the point of view of an exciting-challenging other, and hears all of the subject's own statements through the "reception" and address of the other.

It is only because he strives for nothing more than to think through the deadly seriousness of ontologically ironic subjectivity that Heidegger can, as the outstanding upriser among philoso-phers, feel his way towards a different ontological gesture, one that reclaims the uprising. By looking for the not-rising-up in his thinking in a towering way, he becomes a thinker who "stands" completely in the dubious twilight. One will have to accept that he – to greatness obliged – does not accept responsibility for this twilight as a personal dubiousness or logical ambiguity, but elevates it back into the great text of the happenings of being. If the enframing, the placing upright, was also not our doing, but the destiny of being, so a possible dis-stance will again remain wholly a thing of being and only from out of "this itself" can the page be turned, if that is really necessary. With pride and sorrow, Heidegger's twilight of metaphysics mingles with the dusk of metaphysics that he defined, which probably thinks of itself as the appropriate working environment for the dismantling of the world-historical framing structure that demanded subject dominion, metaphysics, and technology all at the same time. Both gloomy and serene, this thinking takes its solitary exemplary position. It is gloomy because it still carries with it in a forceful gesture the legacy of the history of metaphysical exertion and armament; it is serene because it has repeated and overtaken the huge wave of erecting installations to which it itself belongs, and has already reached a point of détente, at which others can let themselves be intuited as erecting stances. These other stances promise to be restrained and unassuming, but by promising that, they multiply the twilight because they need to emphasize the unemphasized and want the unwanted. Heidegger's ambivalence leaves open the question of whether his thinking continues or ends metaphysics; yes, according to his gesture, it almost parodically and gaudily repeats the metaphysical rising up to prepare its overcoming. There is little concern about whether this overcoming will be thwarted by the pathetic preparation for it. Twilight-like to the core, it conjures up a Titanism of inconspicuousness and opens the horizon with thunder, from which the other approaches on "the feet of doves."[17]

Meanwhile, it seems, the gun smoke over the philosophical battlefield has cleared. After the wound that was Heidegger, the time has come to also perceive the matter that is Heidegger. If it is taken up again, it already pushes beyond the formulation in which the master from the Black Forest left it. I hope we have left no doubt about the direction in which the "question of being," once newly set in motion, strives: towards a theory of birth, a phenomenology of the coming-into-the-world – a new Maieutic, an onto-topology, an onto-kinetics, an onto-politics. From these tendencies one thing becomes clear: it is a revenge on Heidegger since he considered psychology unnecessary and anthropology beneath him. As soon as a psychologically and anthropologically grounded philosophy enters into a meditation of self-born structures, it arrives at a more radical destruction and a more substantive salvation of metaphysical discourses about being and nothingness than Heidegger's memory of being was able to accomplish. For what the history-making intrusion of subjectivity was and is can, according to Heidegger, be sharply reconstructed in a grammar of dramas of self-birth,[18] and the interlocutors who inform us about the categories of self-bringing-forth are the great birth theorists of tradition and current research: Plato and Bloch, Schelling and Rank, Patanjali and Marx, Johannes Climax and Nietzsche, Maine de Biran and Stanislav Grof.

Practical knowledge is provided by the mothers, the midwives, the phenomenologists of bringing forth and carrying. The task of moderating this conversation, of course, can rest with none other than the Master Lao Tzu, the Old Child, who had lived through the risks of becoming to the end, before he, after eighty-one years, as white-haired as an elder and as profound as the world itself, emerged from his mother's womb to take on life on the outside, in the certainty of being, even in the outside world, the same as he was while inside. In his world-superior serenity, the question for us is what else are the self-birthing struggles of historical humanity other than efforts to compensate for the disadvantage of all disadvantages, the "disadvantage of having being born." (Emil Cioran is the most eloquent witness of this in the twentieth century, alongside Beckett.)

As a school of coming-into-the-world, philosophy really enters into the post-metaphysical "basic position," which it has been demanding for two hundred years with great noise and insufficient arguments. From this new (even pre-Socratic and gynecological) basic position, philosophy is at the end and the beginning at the same time; it has its story behind it and at the same time before it; it has both failed as an attempt to come into the world, and has not even seriously begun with it. In vain and unceasingly, it remains thrown back to the effort-that-it-is. Because effort is at the core of subjectivity, philosophy as a phenomenon of exertion can never get away from subjectivity, no matter what denying, subversive, or suicidal strategies it may still come up with. Its only chance lies in the rise to serenity – but serenity begins with the willingness to allow oneself to be exerted by the real. According to metaphysics, it can take philosophy all the way to humor, the democratic version of divine madness. Beyond exertion, there remains only exertion to overcome exertion. Philosophy, for now, can do nothing better than confront its destiny of being the logical pinnacle of subjectivity at the most exciting, exhausting, and crazy places. It must reenact its history in order to understand what it was and is, and in this way stand, in solidarity with its hybrids as well as its tragic stances, its misguided and its inevitable gestures. If rigor still has a purpose in this questionable discipline, then it is to think oneself into the surge of the most extreme exertion in order to ascertain the limits of exertion.

Subjectivity, we said, is kinetically the effort-that-I-am. The limits of my effort are the limits of my stance, the limits of my standing of my ground, my persevering, enduring, maintaining, entertaining. Where the effort ends, there the standing upright comes to its limit on its own, that is where that which "lies otherwise than this" begins. Perhaps "the other" in that sense is just a term for what lies down while we stand upright – even possibly what we need to actively make to underlie in order to have something for our standing upright to stand on. For the subject there lies behind its limit at first only that which falls victim to exhaustion: the subject self – in the mode of collapse. Overtired, overwhelmed, devastated, it encounters itself yet again beyond its own limit. There, its stances prove untenable and its promises baseless. The uncanny place in the forest from which the hero on his tree sees nothingness eating itself forward is none other than the place the sight of which is unbearable to the eye of the subject, because it shows that, with all its efforts, the subject is literally nothing in the end. Nothingness is the manifestly progressive untenability of the promised, it is the leaching of everything that exists into a holding device for stances long recognized as untenable. This is the surge of life fatigue that rolls over the dams of broken promises, making the bodies as heavy as their own burial plates. This nothingness protrudes into the self-experience of the overexerted subject when it comes to the limits of its standing its ground. It is only through the fully endured overload that the subject gets to where it can see through its Great Orthopedics. What no external criticism can tell it, it learns of the symptoms of its own overexertion. Only too late does it understand that it has set up the world as a device for keeping untenable promises, and from then on it finds itself in danger of being slain by the collapse of these buildings that are as enormous as they are unstable. Even greater is the danger of drowning in one's "adult" stance – that's Neo-Stoicism – or, at the first regressive liberalization, exploding into murderous disinhibitions – that's fascism.

In the disintegration of its stances, the subject comprehends how all its self-birthing stances depend on guidelines that elude its independence. In collapse, it approaches the "ground" that underlies all installations. In this approach, it makes acquaintance with what psychiatrists call the chance of depression. The remark that even an upright stance is just a lying down in an unlikely bed corresponds to this. Lying down, however, is another term for the kinetic pattern of serenity: letting oneself be carried. What Heidegger lamented with enormous effort as "forgetting of being" corresponds to a forgetting of letting oneself be carried within the kinetic consciousness, which is a precondition of every rage of self-reliance. However, this forgetting is not an actual forgetting; it springs from the memory of the body in the real episodes where it experienced itself as being not carried, abandoned, forgotten, and imprisoned in its own despair – of the moments in which it accumulated the most unforgettable motivations to stand on its own. But however deep the forgetting of letting oneself be carried and its recoil towards self-uprising, even the most extreme rage of self-birth can make of itself no more than what the first birth has already made of it: a being who always hovers in danger, even if it is a self-created one. The first and second births agree that they bring into the world living beings who, as beings who exert themselves, strive for self-protection, but who, at the end of the day, can achieve nothing better than to accept themselves as the hovering beings that they have always been and still are. This is the chance of depression. You have to get on the ground to learn that it has a double bottom. Those who come from untenable standing to lying down cannot be far from learning that lying down is just another kind of hovering.

At the turning point between the subject's extreme self-establishment and its plunge into a carried hovering lies a passage for
which Heidegger introduced the ominous word "turn," a word
supposed to form a common denominator for both the giganto-
mania of Meßkirch and the history of the European spirit – how
could it not if, after millennia of self-forgetfulness, being was in the
mood to choose the musings of this man as the stage of its own
self-remembrance.

There is nothing to the word "turn" and its religious reverber-
ation. What is essential about it is the reference to the movement
through which the wave of the subject's force runs back into itself.
This movement would be impossible without the gentle counter-
violence of failure. But anyone who speaks of a "turn" thinks
of failure not as a mere collapse, not just as entropy, which puts
an end to an unlikely state, but as a "sign" from the other side.
Those who hear it and look in its direction have already allowed
themselves to be turned around and made a movement away from
the wrong movement. Such a turnaround is more than a mechanical
change of direction, nor does it have anything to do with what the
installation technicians of the New Age call switching to "complex
thinking." The turning process would precisely not be a future-
greedy continued muddling under new auspices, but an ontological
ebb of subjectivity; but the ebb is not made, it only occurs when the
tide changes its mind. If we take the tide as an image for the exertion-
that-we-are which we cannot refrain from, it becomes clear that a
returning tide kinetically remains a thing of impossibility as long as
the waves of exertion have not dissipated of their own accord and
been used up. Here, the thrill of the danger into which the project
of modernity has led us makes itself palpable on an ontological
level: anything less than a change in the meaning of "being" will
not suffice for our "salvation." Because modernity is in its process
nothing other than being-towards-movement, movement towards
movement in increasing loops of self-intensification, our survival is
tied to a self-withdrawal of the kinetic tidal wave "within us." This
cannot be changed with external canalization and decelerations. A
critical movement can only emerge from the self-absorbing of the
mobilization wave if it has thrown itself forward to its critical point.
For us, however, it cannot even be considered that such a critical
point "exists" – certainly, there "is" no such point in the sense of an
external threshold, a "line," which one only has to cross in order to
romp in a neo-positive way of being. If such a point exists and if it
actually occurs, then initially it is only so that the mobilizing fury of
individual subjects ebbs away – whether it has exhausted itself, it has
collapsed through sudden twists, or the élan of the subject has taken

leave of its expenditure in trivial motor skills in order to instead reach "yogic" or artistic heights. It would be unwise, though, to deny the unpredictable in the emergence of such turning points – as unwise as are the thought patterns that circulate today that directly run from danger to salvation and from a hopeless world situation to a logic of salvation. Even if salvation existed for us, it would not be logical, but cyclical, not the product of necessity, but a gift of opportunity. Those who promise themselves anything more are only making use of auto-hypnotic forces; they mobilize the wonderful ability to deceive themselves as much as they think it necessary to live. But aren't those days over, when auto-hypnotists were allowed to act like philosophers of history?

Let us presuppose: there is no detectable point of "turnaround" and no necessary and sufficient conditions for it. But there are twists and turns that we cannot create ourselves which place themselves on unpredictable points of the curve of action.

"Turn" could be the title for the subject's relaxation from its self-birthing overstretches. It would then refer to the transition from a way of being determined to do everything to one serene towards some things. Of course, the transition to serenity itself is something that cannot make a serene impression. In transition, the fragility of the world is exposed. The powers that have piled themselves up in the enframing of civilization breathe a fatal breeze towards us through the membrane of a soft consciousness. Just as the warm Alpine wind draws the mountains to the front of the city limits, serenity exposes the panorama of the world to be pure explosiveness. If there is an active part in the turn, it is one of precaution against the destructiveness that is unleashed in the collapse of untenable positions. The serenity leads not only out of false efforts, but even more so away from the false alleviations of the mobilization processes.

Serenity grows out of the advantage of not having won. It resembles defeat in a fight that would be a disaster to win. Those whom it reels in feel a relaxation from the struggle with the struggle, from the sting of subjectification, which crumbles more into itself the more it tries to raise itself upright. Serenity colors the self-knowledge of the subject who knows what it is like to have tired oneself out on the impossible. While the self-birth of the subject is the eternal agony and, as the engine of history, also represents the grotesque attempt we cannot refrain from to come to a world of our own through our own power, the serene dependence upon our first birth leads to the rediscovery of the inevitable. It could be that this discovery presupposes the odyssey of subjectivity. On a big journey, one tends to spin and wear out stories of self-reliance and self-preservation. Perhaps the inevitable shimmers through the thinly woven threads of one's "own" will, from which the subject drifts away on its way to the exit with fateful force. Wasn't subjectivity the effort to bypass the inevitable? Thus, at the end of its being completely worn out and used up, the subject becomes transparent to itself as an indefensible and at the same time indissoluble fiction – some say in the form of a divine lie. One rubs one's eyes and becomes acquainted with the inevitable.

Once again, we must return to Heidegger, for it is he who made the remembering of the "inevitable" into an explicit topic. (However, one may suspect that it was not the inevitable that interested him, but "inevitability," because he was after all a philosopher whom metaphysics held in its grasp, and, as such, has incorrigibly fallen prey to generalities.) When Heidegger proclaims in one of his most whispering speeches the phrase that people would first have to become "mortals," he arrives, banished to the classical metaphysical questions, only at the weaker inevitability, at least in comparison with the first and strongest inevitability that people must first become those who are born, those who come into the world. What they have always been the most is what they are the least at the end. Frightened and fascinated by their mortality, they look beyond birth as well as beyond what is most incidental. The cogito of death has stifled even the smallest approach to a cogito of birth – to Heidegger and to this day.[19]

But if the age of metaphysics were to really end, it would not be the I-die that must be able to accompany all my ideas, but the I-come-into-the-world. A post-metaphysical devotion of thought to the finite earth cannot be marked by mortality, which forever remains a motive of metaphysical temptation, but must only be marked by the sign of birth. Because it is not enough for people to be born; in order to come into the world, they are condemned to see themselves as arrived beings – beings who cannot yet be ascertained because they have not yet come into the world, and whose every attempt to nevertheless ascertain themselves is doomed. The most radical self-recognition of human beings refers not to the fact that they refuse to recognize that they will die, but to their evasion of the idea "I-was-born" in a panicked flight. No one wants to have been present at the event that brought them to the light of the world. Being born – that only happens to other people.[20]

No one, it seems, remembers their entry into the world, though, in terms of the physiology of memory, there is nothing that should prevent us from visualizing even the most archaic event. So here we "are," and no one knows how. When we start talking about things of this world "in the world," our sentences begin in the middle, subsequently, straggling, without direct insight into how we managed to get to where we are.

But however much we talk and reflect, no talk, no reflection cancels out the fact that our utterances are overtaken by birth and released only by birth. This darkness of birth, which serves as a foil for all knowledge, is not an innocent not-yet-being-acquainted with something new. It is a constitutive not knowing, a darkness as the first intention. The forgetting of birth is a well-established non-knowledge that provides the fundamental effort to self-formation: not to have been there. Only when the subject reaches the limit of its erection efforts can it extract from its exhaustion the otherwise unacceptable and feel its origin in the fright of birth, in the falling out and staying lying down, in the feeling of being too heavy for itself. As soon as the defensive tension of self-birthing crumbles, an inner flow gets under way, trickling old self-knowledge of the first birth into the present. The more presently a life takes place, the lower its amount of effort towards misunderstanding in relation to its birth dowry. On the abyssal ground of the present, the ex-subject can retrospectively comprehend what its "true nature" was: the urge not to have nature; the drive to crush the stepmotherly earth beneath oneself; the tension of getting out of the suffocating, abused downsizing as a motherless self-birther. These energies are what make history. Everything that is considered a subject in this specific sense contributes to the great world text that appears under the title My, Your, His, Our, Their Struggle. It is about miscarriage into a false world and rebirth into a proper one, it is about heroic exodus and crusades through time, missions and time turns, last battles, projects of modernity and the final realms of self-government – however, the "last" chapters are always written by those who have somehow escaped the catastrophes of the subject. Will there be someone to tell of our struggle, too?

Because, following philosophical tradition, we have characterized the path of subjectivity as an odyssey-like cycle into an unfamiliar starting point, the impression could now arise that the simplest things must always and inevitably only emerge at the end of a long expedition. From here, one could infer that the mind has a necessity to go on detours. For the kind of thinking that has come under the metaphysical compulsion to exert itself, this is actually true: the subject's path to the world has the structure of a detour into the elementary. On it, the inevitable and the self-evident appear last. And as long as philosophy is embroiled in the drama of the subject's self-birthing efforts, it seems doomed to always opt for the longest detour as the shortest route to things. Where heroes think, there the long road is the only reasonable one; for them, overexertion is the minimum contribution.

Is there no alternative to this? Do only tired heroes have the final say after returning home from the colonies? Is the inevitable always such that those who avoid it always encounter it at the last minute anyway? No – there is another beginning of conscious life that has not ended up on the long road through history. But this other consciousness has found no forceful advocates – except in marginal literature. Only today, in contrast to heroic thinking, which only admits the self-evident too late and at the last minute, can an unheroic consciousness come into its own, which does not win its insights on a detour across the path of maximal misunderstanding of that which is most simple. Like Hercules at a crossroads, human consciousness has a choice from the beginning between the short and the long way, between the odyssey and the stroll, and even if the choice must first fall on the long route, because self-birthers, who burst with their compulsion to strength, do not know what else to do with themselves other than to overexert themselves, that does not mean our right to take the short way has been denied. This right is known to a hidden tradition, a tradition unaffiliated with any faculties, especially law faculties, to speak nothing of philo-sophical ones. To remind us of this right is the metaphysical-critical purpose of the confrontation between the great thinker Plato and the gutter-level mime artist, Diogenes, as we have learned from Greek anecdote. As a philosopher, the clown shows the philoso-phers that there is an alternative to the spiritual heroic ascent into the life of ideas. Even divine mania has a more popular variation. The other way out of the overexertion is to not enter into it – the enlightened beggar from Sinope has demonstrated how this can be done. From his cynical impulse, discreet and denigrated traces of pre-metaphysical wisdom run through the age of metaphysics and the philosophy of the subject, to become more conspicuous and self-confident again at their twilight. Just as in the uprising period of metaphysics, the other consciousness retreated into pantomime, literature, comedy, and quiescence, so in its time of collapse the voices of wisdom become audible again. They are the voices of the oldest dissidence; they belong to women, children, ecstatics, rogues, inconspicuous people – people who don't let themselves be persuaded that they were not there when they came into the world. No, they were there. Whatever happens to them meets their amazement. They know in their own way what it means to come out into the uncanny; without a metaphysical fishing net, they balance across everyday cliffs. From them, the down-and-out subject can learn the self-evident that indeed arrives last "before its eyes" and "to its ears."

Eurotaoism

He who stands on tiptoe is not steady.
He who strides cannot maintain the pace.

Tao Te Ching, 24[21]

The Eurotao that can be spoken is not the real Eurotao, etc.

4

THE FUNDAMENTAL AND THE URGENT – OR: THE TAO OF POLITICS

Also a contribution to the answer as to why a credible politics currently does not exist

Difficile est satyram non scribere.

Juvenal, *The Satires*[1]

Americans are surely to be envied. If a writer in the United States who was rumored to belong to an alternative movement were invited into political circles to initiate a conversation about opposing worldviews (literary supplements might appreciate this), then that writer would bring a manuscript that gloriously displayed the words THE TAO OF POLITICS on its title page, and everyone among those involved would think it perfectly fine for this person to use the tools at their disposal. Even in the choice of words, the message would be clear – Good morning, America, welcome to the New Age where a young Aquarian ease converses with the old fishy severity of reality; the End of World War, the Beginning of Intercontinental Eroticism! – and hardly anyone would take offense at the esoteric wink across the Pacific towards Old China, where, as we know, there are so many sages that only one child per family is allowed in order to stop the rush towards the bosom of enlightenment – it is rumored that these days, only the billionth young Taoist sees the light of day.

Old Europe is having a harder time, and a writer who has discussions with politicians has a harder time here, too. There is no trace of transatlantic relaxation and no talk of the Tao of politics. Here, Protestant ethics are still intact; in Bonn, there is a tough negotiation on the matter. Mr Johannes Rau[2] will present his political moral doctrine in a forward-looking keynote speech and then the invited author will give his lecture. The organizer has left no doubt as to the subject on which he wishes statements to be made: "Of the possibility and difficulties of *credibly* embodying political principles in everyday operations." This is how an officer of the hosting foundation has formulated the impressive problem, and it must be admitted that the question is quite deliberate. Political morality is at stake and how to avoid the mistake of having too much of it – we are in the territory of classical social democracy. The thought of the "embodiment" of principles is ominously surrounded with precautions. One suspects that in the race between the difficulties and the possibilities, the difficulties will be at the forefront, but that does not disturb us; we are all adults here. (Klaus Staeck, who is also on the podium, will immediately swear to the party's capacity for suffering, and Paul Lorenzen, who is sitting in the audience, will afterwards, while on the floor, emphasize his inability to be shocked by anything the author says.[3])

What to do among only adults? At first, nothing remains for me but an escape into confession, and so I unreservedly admit that such subjects make me feel embarrassed or, what is even more frustrating, listless. I would rather be in America. No, staying here, holding our ground, life will make men out of us. Listlessness, who do you think you are – what kind of category is that in the first place? Whatever it may be as a category, it is now above all an acute fact. The assertion that in my case we are dealing with a post-modern listlessness does not help either. As you know, post-modern is what we call the hopelessness that can no longer even be originally formulated. Modernity has exhausted all the possibilities of formulating enlightened displeasure with the world, and even condemned us to cite sources when it comes to the most recent annoyances. For generations now, everything has already been said about the incongruity between morality and politics; even cynical summaries of the state of affairs have long been part of the classical repertoire. It is not possible to act as if discoveries can be made in these matters. It is already a standard self-interpretation of modernity that the political course of the world is moving ever further away from what is morally correct. After all, I belong to a generation whose philosophically formative impressions included Adorno's thesis that the whole is the false – more formative, however, was Liza Minnelli's thesis that life is a cabaret. In direct comparison with Adorno's, Minelli's theorem seems to have the advantage by seeing irony as something built into the world and does not assume a subject that has brought irony into it. Why still make jokes when we are the joke? It should be mentioned that since 1917 philosophy has only been possible in the form of Dadaism – but after the latter has done its job as far as it is concerned, its trainees have to try to live up to the bloody seriousness of what is no longer to be taken seriously using new means. Philosophers of today – what else are they other than experts for the reformulating of jokes back into problems? The embodiment of moral principles in political action? This, too, becomes a philosophical problem on request; only do not forget that today philosophizing means making the effort not to write satire.

After these remarks, you have the right to ask what I was doing at such a serious event. You will not even engage with the sophism that you can only seek what you bring to the table; that is understandable. But the reference to bringing something is nevertheless legitimate, because what I bring in my luggage is the arch-romantic prejudice that an embarrassment can also be an opportunity. If I here take over the supplementary lecture to Mr Rau's expositions on political credibility, then a dose of occasionalism is at play – by the way, it is a matter less alien to Mr Rau than one might assume when one considers politics only as a fulfillment of duty towards the fatherland on the energy and pension front. He is, after all, a candidate for chancellor (we write in January 1986; the blue flower of the absolute majority for our candidate's party still blooms), someone who, in his own way, gathers experience with the genius of opportunity. Aren't candidacies the poetic periods of political life, simply because, as long as they last, one may not yet commit the sins that are preprogrammed into the prose of administration of office? *Candidati*, one recalls, was, according to the Roman state ritual, the name of the men dressed in white who indicated a willingness to lose their innocence by putting on an untarnished robe – they were brides of the principle of reality, whose defloration potential has been legendary since those ancient days. In the given case, no one would go so far as to dress the candidate for a political wedding in white since his national political experience is up to date on file; even on the dubious terrain of political morality, no one can define how often someone may have lost their innocence until they can no longer be considered a beginner. Malicious gossip has still not stopped claiming that one can see a dark stain from the emissions of the Ibbenbüren power plant showing through the white candidate robe of Mr Rau, so black that no new integrity can emerge against the accumulated sins. But we are not here to moralize. Perhaps a candidate's white signals more today than a non-binding ritual – namely the willingness to expose oneself to a change of mind that gives the present moment in world history its philosophical profile.

And that is the code word that gives our intervention its cue. Today, there are not only partisan occasions, but dramatic global reasons to speak of such changes in attitude. The boundless incongruity that gapes open between the competences of politics and the requirements of reality give us food for thought. At the moment, no one knows how the apocalyptic tendencies of the system could be brought within the range of preventative measures. Politics has turned into a game of blind man's buff to the highest degree right before our eyes – but because the players hardly ever let themselves be caught, politics cannot take off the blindfold. Everyone can tell that in this children's game with reality, the danger increases, and if we speak of the principles of politics, we may talk of morality but what we really mean is danger. One aspect of the danger in which we float as both subjects and objects of politics consists not least in the reduction of amoral risks to moral questions to appease the vulnerable. If nothing else, an objection from a philosophical perspective must be directed against it on this forum. A philosophy of the real speaks of reality as dangerousness, and of the fact that danger manifests itself today not least in the dissonance between the fundamental and the urgent. This dissonance will be the topic of what follows.

Should we wish to characterize the dangerousness of the present philosophically, we must choose an offensive diagnosis and realize that the epochal strategy of excluding questions of truth from the political sphere and from the civilizing process (now one's teeth become loose) has altogether hit a limit. The return of the excluded is being foreshadowed in a series of symptomatic catastrophes. They present a tough bill to the truth-abandoned activism of modernity. If there is a common denominator for the multitude of crises that have fissured contemporary consciousness, it can be found in the open secret that is given away by the catastrophes: the modern myth of praxis is dying and occidental activism is experiencing its twilight of the idols. But we would be underestimating praxis as a principle if we were to see it as governed merely by ideology. If that is all it was, it would never have unleashed its world-moving power. The modern theory-supported and morality-flanked praxis was, after all, able to tease out latent traits of existence into the open and displace seemingly unshakeable structures of reality. The practicistic *mythos* of modernity is nothing less than a universally claimed exegesis of being. It owes its revolutionary assertiveness to the authority of scientific technology; it owes its feats and its psycho-political attractiveness to the advantages of an individualistic ethics of expression whose doctrine is "better to act than to suffer." All the mobilizations that shape the face of modernity in the economic, technological, scientific, military, legal, and informational field come together in the phenomenon of practicism. In this particular sense, praxis is really a praxis of change and mobilization; an attack on the given, a will to penetration, dissolution, transformation, and a movement towards increasing mobility. All these mobilizations draw their epistemological motives[4] from the conceptual Basic Decisions of the metaphysical tradition, and in particular from the younger Enlightenment's deployment of the difference between light and matter into a relationship between work and substance.

Enlightenment, one might say, is metaphysics of light turned aggressive, organizing itself as an trans-illuminating offensive that advances with unprecedented force across the natural limits of exposure to light up the previously unlit interior of things and make it available. In the name of the Enlightenment, the Old European metaphysics of light moves to a pragmatic stage where the cross-millennial movement evolves from the initial contemplative view of the illuminated to the final irradiation of objects. Irradiation means annihilation – reduction, release, transformation, mobilization. It does not take a genius to see that mobilizations become explosions once they pass a certain threshold. To the extent that loud bangs and crashes can currently be heard from all four corners of the world simultaneously, we can no longer hide our doubts about the durability of modernity. The spreading critique of Western practicisim is therefore not an irrationalism, as interested circles proclaim everywhere nowadays. (Some seem to be of the opinion that we must protect praxis from theory.) No, this criticism soberly challenges us to deal with the hypothesis that all the great risks of the present are based in rationally predictable mobilization disasters.

This preliminary sketch of an alternative "philosophical discourse of the present" remains laconic. It merely indicates what is at stake in current fundamental reflections. It would be superficial to talk about any partial crisis such as, for example, the loss of political credibility with respect to the population without also providing a more radical general diagnosis. Only by participating in the creation of such diagnostics could the political actors prevent themselves from being bad contemporaries. And this is precisely – let us be honest – what we must consider the vast majority of them to be. This is where the crisis of political credibility originates in the first place. Even the dullest members of the public (to say nothing of the reflective ones) get a disastrous impression from the behavior of the political class insofar as this exhibits nothing more than the most hopeless carrying on, abandoned by all spirits, both good and evil – the uncoiling of a phantom-like, unbroken practicism that is cut off from the development of a more sensible awareness ("out there" in society) of the problem. Credibility, if not that of politics but certainly that of the politician, could therefore only be rehabilitated from this perspective. At the end of the day, it does not matter if this or that politician has a personality type well suited for power, if they belong to this or that party, if they care more about the interests of workers than those of bank capital, if they cultivate the community of values with people of good will on church days, if they wrestle for their briefcase with prostitutes in front of New York hotels: these are all pardonable sins or secondary virtues. What it comes down to is whether a politician can qualify as the subject of an advanced awareness of the problem. A politician who could offer this would have fulfilled all suitable requirements and be forgiven for occupational sins. But no one will claim that Bonn and other capitals are teeming with such political light bearers. This cannot be – already because a gap of sensitivity opens up in modern societies where the political class and the problem-sensitive aesthetic subcultures become hopelessly estranged from each other. It is impossible to close one's eyes to the fact that there is a deadly division of labor between the sensible and the resilient: a division for which deeper reasons are probably responsible than just the draining effect of the political fourteen-hour day. It is probably not organically economically possible to live on the edge (more precisely, to set up one's office on it) and examine it at the same time. In any case, ever since Walther Rathenau, German politics has not seen another case where political intelligence, aesthetic perceptiveness, capacity for sociological analysis, and philosophical reflection were all united in a high-ranking leader. Despite that, we must not let anything less than the unlikely have validity in this field. To speak credibly about credibility, it is necessary to clarify what its substantial criterion would consist of. When it comes to such matters, lowering one's expectations from the very beginning would mean rationalizing a bankruptcy that has already taken place.

Below, the topic will be unfolded in three directions or phases. First, we will take up the notorious "credibility gap" that was discovered by political semanticists a few years ago and brought into the discussion – a phenomenon that has probably worked its way both into the vocabulary and the self-perception of political upper echelons with some stubbornness. Following that, we will pursue the philosophical assumptions underlying the idea that principles can be embodied in everyday operations. We end with a few sentences stating that it would be both advisable and due to liquidate the ethics of principles into an ethics of urgency.

Dimensions of the Credibility Gap

A gap and its dimensions? Here it is in cold print, but it should be noted that the obliqueness of the expression has been consciously accepted because it corresponds to the structure of the phenomenon itself (insofar as obliqueness is aesthetically homologous to being suspect). Initially, it should be established: the clever term "credibility gap" has so easily been able to win a place in political vocabulary in the last few years because they were the years when system-theoretical, marketing-strategic, and theatrical categories overturned the field of moral-political "discourses" without encountering hardly any resistance.

From now on, we not only have to deal with information gaps, energy gaps, the Fulda Gap (preferred gate of entry for Russian armored forces), market gaps, and technology gaps, but also with ethical gaps such as that of credibility or predictability which act as the field of operations of interaction technologies. Whoever embraces this linguistic prescription shows they have understood the basic rule of pragmatism: the management of a problem is to be considered its solution until further notice. Thus, the essential political talent proves to be the ability to make yourself comfortable in a deplorable state of affairs. And if we speak of the "dimensions" of the credibility gap, then deficiency is point-blank positivized: it is no longer a deficit, but a market. From then on, we are no longer to understand the gap as a torn hole in material or as a distance between two parameters – rather, it is an independent phenomenon. This positivization also has an advantageous effect, as it tends to occur with some productive demoralizations. It helps by integrating a critical potential into the very description of the matter from its outset. A kind of resistance forces itself between the substance (politics) and the attribute (credible) that no longer allows smooth connections to emerge. Credible politics would amount to a round square. (At this point, the chin of the correspondent of a Hamburg daily newspaper drops to his chest with discouragement; for him, the morning is lost, for this is not the kind of language that keeps us going.) To give an example, the most credible policy today is without doubt that of the Iranian Ayatollahs, since the discrepancy between what politicians are and what they do is nowhere else in the world as trivial as it is there. They are by far the most characterful, credible politicians of our time. Compared to them, the newer Chinese politics, for example, is almost shockingly unreliable, volatile, and, in a fascinating way, devoid of character.

One can understand, of course, why Western professional politicians (who are tired of the chronic doubt being cast on their morality) have originated the fantasy that the credibility gap ought to be closed. For once, they would like to see the currents of approval flow unbroken from the governed to the rulers; they dream of being a pure medium of the people just once in their lives and of embodying a credible, undiluted emanation of common interests.

They balk at the morally precarious insight that the lack of credibility as such is constitutive of the modern concept of politics as a whole. Regardless of their reservations against it, we must insist, based on the law of the matter, that credibility is only possible for modern politics in the form of a disclosure of the stipulations of its incredibility.

Hereto belongs a history lesson. Since the age of absolutism – more precisely, since the regicidal phase of the French Revolution – political rule in the West has been gradually de-sacralized. From that point on, political power has stood less in the light shining from above and more under the pressure of approval from below. Such a change in the very basis of legitimacy has been accompanied by a profound transformation of how power and rule are enacted. It can be recognized in the form of an increasing depersonalization of power, bureaucratization of politics, and prioritizing of decision-making procedures over the acute urgency of problems. In this way, power has become more diffuse and more indirect, on the one hand, and more penetrating and ubiquitous, on the other. These are banalities, but they clarify why it has become difficult to see political events under a transfiguring or some other kind of "higher" light. The secularization of the political has liquidated the reserves of romantic loyalty and patriarchal attachment that may have existed between the authorities and populations in the age of direct rule. As its secular and rational distinguishing feature, modernity does not allow for a sacral-political restoration.

The political realm is now either a sober workplace or a battlefield for those who manage to format their existential passions into practical "interests." According to a modern understanding, politics is what remains when passions are excluded and pushed into the religious, aesthetic, and erotic districts of the "private." It is only through this drastic modification that people can be turned into political subjects of the modern kind: only when they reduce themselves from beings who have passions to subjects who have interests will they attain the status of political persons. One can assume that the roots of any unease at the "lack of credibility" in politics are to be sought in the anthropological stylization of *homo politicus* as a modern subject of interest. For the individual can only become a political subject to the extent that they are able to refrain from what gives their existence the "authentic", the "credible" trait. What modernity calls "the political" only appears by neutralizing what is existentially most important. Emerging from repression, politics must at the same time impose itself as the most important surrogate for that which is most important. It can only succeed insofar as it ensures that nothing else becomes more important than politics. For this reason, politics is, as Bismarck claimed, the art of the possible, the art of the next best – its passion is the neutralization of passions. Such a definition of politics as "statesmanship" can be traced back to the absolutist age, when the early modern state began to establish itself as a meta-absolutism of a special kind over the militantly absolutized religious passions and creeds. Where the mortal god, as Hobbes defined the modern state, established his regiment, confessions of faith and passions become neutralized into private matters and should under no permissible circumstances come into question as the *causae belli*, especially when it comes to civil wars. (One can verify the validity of this rule by the exceptions of Northern Ireland or Lebanon that prove it – both cases of unsuccessful neutralization of passions and failed politicization or funding of "interests.") The political double figure of the sovereign and the subject has been in effect ever since absolutism – it lives on in the legal figure of the citizen, where moments of subjection and sovereignty are made into a kind of self-subjection. The citizen of the state is the political figure in whose "own interest" it is to have political interests and not passions.

It is precisely because passions must be privatized and neutralized in the political culture of modern times that the corresponding political subjects are constitutionally abstract. In this fact, the political achievement of modernity and its greatest weakness become one and the same: although its social systems are built upon abstraction from passions, they are forced to produce a passion for the abstract in a deeply paradoxical way – otherwise, the psychosocial brackets that are supposed to hold the great systems together would immediately break apart. But warming people to the cold will always be a problematic endeavor in the long run. One might get the impression that this is an alchemist piece of art that the anthropological equipment of *homo sapiens sapiens* has not provided for (but perhaps another *sapiens* is yet to be added). Exceptions to these paradoxes can be divided into only two groups: those who are engaged in politics as a profession and cannot fail to place any private passions they still might have at the service of the profession as a subjective subsidy; and those who passionately and aggressively engage in acute political issues as laymen. When this happens, passions are no longer private and political scientists speak of "social movements." It is not for nothing that this expression has alarming connotations; it reminds us that what is "most important" can return to the political arena at any time. Indeed, social movements prove that the modern reduction of passions to interests is an anthropologically unstable operation that can be thrown into question overnight by so-called "fundamentalist" upheavals. Career politicians are naturally suspicious of such fundamentalism; for the rules of the game in their profession are that people do not have fundamental beliefs but rather principles, not passions but interests, not axioms but options.

Thus, whoever wishes to study the credibility gap where it originally opens up must understand how the modern political subject comes into being through a reduction of the self into the representation of interests and civic self-subjugation. And because individuals would eventually atrophy within such reductions, compensations are vitally important. Within existential jargon, such compensations are called engagements. (Engagement is passion in the form of decision.) The only paths open to engagement lead either to professionalism or to fundamentalism – both forms of compensation are rightly perceived as something even less credible than what they are supposed to aid in becoming more credible. By categorially dividing the political class into doers and eccentrics, we instinctively identify the two great variants of modern political lack of credibility. The primary dimension of the credibility gap, we claim, is therefore not the so-called "alienation" of politics from the "authentic interests of the population," as trivial political scientists would have us believe, but the alienation of the population from their passions in favor of those interests that are implanted in them like an artificial heart – and, incidentally, these are almost always the interests in mobilizations. The primary problem is not that institutions become independent and separate themselves from the grass roots but that the grass roots separate themselves from themselves in order to participate as political subjects in the mobilization project of the modern age. Therefore, credibility is primarily an issue not of political ethics but of political anthropology. On the other hand, explaining the credibility gap as caused by the alienation between politicians and the population only captures its secondary dimension. No one will deny that this, too, has its pitfalls and can be a source of unease with respect to politics. But compared to the anthropologically consequential transformation of individuals into politically interested subjects, the fact that there can be no purely representational relationship between so-called "mandates" and political offices because the idiosyncrasies of the offices undermine pure representation is a comparatively harmless phenomenon. Since everyone in the political world theater is their own Member of Parliament who tries to represent their own interests, it is to their benefit to have optimal representatives of those interests. But as long as politics is constituted by the exclusion of what is most important, the bland aftertaste of all actions in the spirit of advocacy cannot be eliminated. The people whose interests are represented look into a mirror when they look at their representative and self-knowledge comes into play when the person looking back at them does not elicit enthusiasm. With an inimitable mixture of subservient suspicion and gloating disdain, they observe the dealings of the political class that represents their rightful representatives. If politicians are almost always unpopular, it's not because they are alienated from the people, but because they are the spitting image of them. The people are rarely so deluded as to find themselves popular. If they are at their wits' end when it comes to themselves, they will vote for those infallibly guaranteed to sink them even deeper into this state. This is precisely what makes up the psycho-political secret of neo-conservative regimes currently predominant in almost the entire Western world. They accurately reflect back the reaction of collective flight into "carry on as usual" where the dumbfounded majorities of interested voters have established themselves. Arm in arm with these majorities, neo-conservatism has opened up an age of political unsavoriness; it has enforced its own inability to be shocked by itself as official etiquette. But its popularity cannot be separated from its simultaneous unpopularity. It finds voter majorities because they find a predictable lack of credibility in it. The public always has the most reasons to consider politicians untrustworthy when they are the way the public wants them to be. As long as they adequately represent the people as they are, politicians will be as untrustworthy as the people are. Whoever governs in the name of the people reduces one's mandate to an indefinable, unstable, fluctuating something that is disinterested in anything but interests; this something periodically lends clear expression to its confusion through general, free, equal, and secret elections. The downfall of people's representatives is not that they stray too far from the people; rather, it is because they do not distance themselves far enough that they are unable to prioritize their receptivity to what is urgent over their interest in interests. Politics is always too close to the citizens, too close to people who stand next to each other for miles in order to represent themselves optimally – to the right of the inevitable, to the right of death and life.

The Voting Voice and the Body – or: How Politics Participates in the Crisis of Embodiment Metaphysics

When the credibility deficit enters into the self-confidence of the actors, it is perceived as a lack of "embodiment." We now know why this cannot be otherwise since political subjects constitute themselves as hollow bodies by subtracting their passions, as it were. It is not without reason that the thing that remains after what is most important has been abstracted is called the vote. Those who have gone through politicization retain nothing of themselves other than their vote, which cannot be used to express anything that constitutes the fullness and sting of life. The voice of the vote speaks in rigid monosyllables; it says nothing but yes and no, never talks spontaneously about its life. It reacts to nominations, marks its X on the voting ballot, and remains laconically limited to minimal signs that indicate either agreement or disagreement. The political vote is so closely related to silence that abstention sometimes says more than the casting of a vote, as those who come from people's democracies know, where voting and approval are synonymous. In contrast, the Western right to opposition is praised with good reason as an enrichment of the political vocabulary in the direction of two syllables. But whether the right to vote expresses itself with one syllable or two, it implies in any case the ambivalent imposition on individuals to reconcile all other strings on the bodily instrument of their existence with its political expression, or to silence them. The more sensible members of the political class have therefore tried to initiate an ethical discourse in order to overcome the aphasia that can no longer be hidden. They have an inkling of how important it would be to repair the destruction of language that follows the political reduction of the fullness of expression to a right to vote. In this predicament, the more thoughtful among the politicians have traditionally received aid from classical intellectuals, who, in their capacity as spokespersons for collective contradictions and life experiences, created an existentially dense language. The political intellectual as embodied in figures of the caliber of Jean-Paul Sartre, Heinrich Böll, or Ernesto Cardenal functioned as a political speech therapist in what seemed to be an elapsed era, waging a highly publicized struggle against monosyllabism. It was above all the writers of the Left who tried to inject languages into the public sphere that were meant to be so complex and excessive that even individualized life could recognize itself in them.

At the moment, there is much evidence to suggest that intellectuals are withdrawing from this function – perhaps because times are too dire for naïvety. Unquestionably, we are at present experiencing a kind of twilight of the intellectuals; in this twilight, the bell tolls for the experts together with the simultaneous resignation of the moral generalists. The intelligentsia, the contradictory class, draws new demarcation lines on the map of the real. Not even intellectuals still believe in a common denominator between politics and life, and it was their task to publicly delude themselves about it. Already at the beginning of the 1920s, the writer Hugo Ball spoke of a "new age of catacombs" that was imminent for the intellectuals. Back then, the ironic break in the political making of the future became apparent to this astute critic of the German zeitgeist. While public life was dominated by simulators of vitality who inflated themselves with new realism, new values, and exclamations of the new ages in the style of oops-we-are-alive and the tone of we-are-the-partners-of-destiny, the life of thinking already knew itself to be condemned to an underground existence. Only by becoming inconspicuous and coming to terms with being regarded with contempt by the makers of the future could it help to ensure that anything worthy of life would survive the century's winter at all. It is only with great difficulty that we can shake off the impression that this situation is being repeated today, only in an even sharper and more globalized form than in the 1920s.

Ever since intelligence has withdrawn and reduced its spoken political contribution to a monosyllablic minimum, politicians have been forced to fend for themselves in their attempts to spiritually revitalize their profession. They must now start using their own resources to turn votes back into languages. Among those who are serious about this, you can recognize the better ones by how difficult they find the task to be. If politicized subjects are no longer just to cast their ballots, but to speak, they must transverse the path of abstraction backward to the existential sources of language. It must be acknowledged that this is an arduous road towards something that is almost impossible. Can automatic answering machines be made to give speeches? Can the disembodied political self, even more barren than the anorexic *cogito* of Descartes, be so readily induced to speak as if from human life in all its fullness? It is only in this kind of predicament that the recourse to principles becomes suggestive for those affected. Because once they are "personally embodied," principles seem to remedy the lack of physicality in politics. That is why "principles" act as guarantors of a full personality and an identity with a broad foundation within the discourse of these new political morality seekers. Those who "credibly embody" higher principles thus seem to bring something substantive into the political game which emanates not only the monosyllabism of the voting specter but also an incarnate principle, a piece of individual culture. Those who embody principles have tied weights to themselves; they are gifted with a gravity of character that cannot be blown away so easily and provided with a moral chassis that is not so easily deformed. It is striking that only those politicians become popular (as far as it is possible) who are distinguished by a certain well-meaning gravity and, above all, by an earthy weight that is not lightened with insights. It is as if populations did not want to lose the overview of what their highest leaders embody. Those who exhibit principles want to make themselves predictable in this way – which is a virtue in a sphere where the production of predictability counts as a confidence-building measure. Without a high degree of embodiment-ready inertia, the desired effect cannot be achieved. But where such principled enthusiasm for embodiment-readiness leads is demonstrated to us by the great men and women of politics who meet in Geneva, Iceland, Vienna, and elsewhere to share their inertia with each other. (This was obviously written before the Washington Treaties of December 1987.[5]) They give the impression that political dialogue is just another word for speaking contests between the speech-impaired. Here, the political psychology of the principle of embodiment shows its frightening side, whereby it turns out that we are dealing with not so much a psychological problem as a problem of the logic of power. If the political subject embodies anything at all, it is not so much their own moral principles but the right to exist of their country, party, system, market share. As incarnations of these, politicians' voices and votes are always those of an armed substantiality and a deadly eloquence. If all competing parties in the political arena firmly embody their principles – and they do so with huge budgets – then the weapons systems are the real bearers of the embodiment of principles. They make our values credible and our strength of character compelling. Thus the politician who best embodies their principles is the one who has installed their convictions on launching pads – on the ground and soon also in the sky.

In view of these reflections on the relationship between voice and body in politics that deviate somewhat from the supposed target, something inevitably needs to be said about the metaphysical premises of the term "embodiment." Laying bare these underlying premises evaporates the false sense of harmlessness with which the prevailing political science (in Bonn as well) speaks about principles and their embodiment. One does not immediately realize that this term represents a forgotten concept of Christian Platonism; more precisely, a John-like theologoumenon that has made its way into trivial language games. In the metaphysical tradition, it is said that existence is divided into the high and the low, the fundamental and the incidental, a spiritual and a material sphere. The spiritual sphere is filled with ideas, principles or first causes, divine categories and forces. The material sphere is that of formless matter without any characteristics; it is dark, spiritless, null and void, and must be guided by the higher forces of form. Matter as the substance of form becomes knowable and real only by the light that shines on it; penetrating into the lack of light, light brings forth formed figures with attributes out of the amorphous material. The visibility of the visible is based solely on the light that originates in the idea and shines through substance. We encounter the most consequential application of this metaphysical model in the Christology of the Gospel of John where the realization of ideas is interpreted as the flesh of the word, and in turn as the Incarnation of God. The word becomes flesh – this is the basic scheme of the leading ideas of embodiment and realization that have shaped the actions and productions of the West. Even those who still invoke fundamental embodiment in political action today, whether they are aware of it or not, are indebted to the Platonic Gospel. Occasionally, this extends to an openly claimed political *imitatio* of Christ when some politicians bring themselves into play as the incarnations of the *logos*, especially in the Protestant world. We must urgently hope that Mr Rau will not build his election campaign and that of his party on a John's Gospel of credibility – this would not only be wrong in terms of tactics, but above all ontologically suspect. What happens in such cases has recently been available for examination in Jimmy Carter's US presidency, which has been battered by the conflict between Christology and Machiavellianism. Similar experiences are guaranteed to anyone who enters such office under similar premises. The incarnation from above inevitably leads to demoralization – or martyrdom (two of the most highly underestimated categories by political science, incidentally). Demoralization follows from the predominance of circumstances over principles. Those who consider demoralization to be the greatest evil should not fail to examine the opposite: for where principles are stronger than circumstances – as in ascetic communities, Jacobin subcultures, and totalitarian systems – there, principle enforces its incarnation at the expense of all other lives.

Is it possible for us to think of an alternative to the incarnation of *logos* or the embodying of the principle? We believe that this is the case. This is becoming increasingly evident in current philosophical thinking, and it is this alternative that gives a perspective of the history of ideas and a logical criterion to the manifold attempts at developing something substantially new in the so-called "alternative cultures." In post-metaphysical culture (which would indeed be an alternative), an understanding is beginning to prevail that it is not the word that must become flesh by force if necessary, but that it is enough to create a place where the spontaneous tendencies of the flesh can get a word in edgewise and have their say. It is no longer a question of embodying principles in action in order to thus subject the inert mass to a force of incarnation from above; instead, we are starting to understand (in an increasingly literal way) that the life-process's own momentum is able to shine forth in brilliant self-relation. The concept of embodiment has become caught in the trap of its own violence and is petering away within it – after all, that was the history-making power of metaphysics. But alternative ways of thinking about the body have already changed direction. To express it in a set way: while the logical endpoint of the compulsion to embody principles is a total liquidation of the flesh in favor of the word, endless perspectives on the self-illumination of life emerge within post-metaphysical learning processes. The moralism of thought in the concepts of embodiment is only the appendix of latent necrological metaphysics that drives life towards the point of a deadly realization. Whoever tries decisively enough to think morality and politics from the point of view of the self-relations of intelligent bodies must give up the notion of embodied principles to create space for a self-experience that shines forth in a very different way.

From an Ethics of Principle to an Ethos of the Urgent

> In the duel between yourself and the world, act as second to the world.
>
> Franz Kafka[6]

According to classical tradition, philosophy is the dialogue of the soul with itself. This assumes that the soul is not unanimous but feels a rupture in itself where the conversation partners of this self-dialogue face each other within the interior. A conversation with ourselves can give us the bizarre yet everyday experience that one part of ourselves gets ahead of us, while another is left behind. This state of tension that constitutes the psychological premise of self-reflection is what colloquial language calls having a conscience. The conscience that makes itself felt is *eo ipso* a conscience that is in tension with *de facto* existence. If individuals form a conscience that lets itself be felt, they are ahead of their own reality and can at least occasionally have something that we call a philosophical self-dialogue. Traditionally, the emotional instance that stirs as conscience is perceived as the "innermost voice." As that which is my innermost, however, it can only appear because it behaves towards me as if it were something superior to me (although coming "from me") that precedes my problematic factual essence. Only insofar as I am not only identical to myself, but also superior, am I capable of the kind of self-dialogue where the masterful voice of conscience converses with the babble of affects, calculations, and interests. Conscience functions as a cybernetic or hegemonic organ of the soul that relates the real states of conscious life to the highest terms of self-regulation – in short, to moral ideas.

If there is now talk in Bonn about the credible embodiment of principles in politics, then this formulation borrows from the conscience model from classical moral philosophy. It suggests that the political subject can orient itself not only in its intimate self-perception, but also in its worldly actions according to the scheme of self-conversation, a conversation where the individual consciousness is at once both disciple and master. The conscience would then not only be the auto-communicative regulating instance in the individual's inner dealings with themselves, but also at the same time the seat of a wisdom that is always ahead of all events in the outside world. The belief in political action according to principles makes the bold (and only seemingly conventional) assumption that there is something in the soul which has enabled it in principle to overtake not only itself but also the world "outside." Consequently, consciences would not only be the internal instances of individuals but also the regulative entities of their external dealings.

We have to admit that this is a seductive idea because it promises an unwavering superiority of the highest organ of the soul over so-called "reality." If valid, it would guarantee the possibility of surpassing not only one's empirical inner life but also the course of the world as a whole, and thanks to a treasure of eternal principles, it would be ahead of it once and for all. This kind of autonomous conscience of principles would make us invulnerable against the shock of events and protect us from changes of circumstances. As the world rages on outside and spins uncontrollably in the vortices of mobilization, we can retreat into our inner citadel and immunize ourselves against the course of events by observing the universals that are permanently engraved in our reflective conscience.

One can easily see where such noble speculation turns short-sighted – as shortsighted as it must be to attempt a suspension of thinking at the aesthetic stage before the atrocity of analysis has a chance to overwhelm it. If we critically analyze the phenomenon of conscience, it immediately becomes apparent that it cannot possibly be understood as an autonomous, internal, and world-superior magnitude. Admittedly, it may seem through immanent contemplation that the subject's fundamental features are forever ahead of any possible inner or worldly event. But we only grasp the decisive fact when we take into account that the appearance of conscience is itself an event "in" the world. This event is anything but random – it is not one coincidence among many others but a dramatic incursion of conscience into the world that turns it into a world for conscience.

But this occurrence does not render all further remote eventfulness of the world process irrelevant. A world that contains conscience and is known by conscience is precisely thereby more than a sample collection of events that can be dealt with according to principles of conscience. Since we are always first born into the world and cannot assume to be "in-the-world" forever, our world conscience cannot only live off what is innate to us, acquired by us, and brought in by us. To put it as shockingly as it indeed is, consciences are in the first instance *not* the self-relations of individuals but self-relations of the world, despite the fact that we only consider individuals to be the ontological premises for such world self-relations. The world calls forth differently conscientious individuals at different times if its internal affairs need to regulate problems through the medium of individual consciences.

Such formations of conscience can certainly fail, and they indeed do fail in an overwhelming number of cases. Among other reasons, they fail when individuals do not form any kind of real relationship to the world and refuse to individuate – this is typical in interested parties and people with end-user sentiments for whom individuation must be the exception to the rule. But the formation of conscience as a relationship to the world also fails if individuals fixate on principles to let the urgent run aground on the fundamental. The keyword here is (yet again) neo-conservatism. What is it other than the mobilization of old principles against new sensibilities? What else does it provide than a cynical desensitizing against the imperative for new forms of conscience that have become crucial in the face of unprecedented dangers? It remains to be seen if social-democratic and socialist parties will take part in such desensitizing under the guise of morality. These have always been the most strongly ambivalent political parties in these matters: on the one hand, because they react relatively sensitively to the development of new practical imperatives – that is part of their tradition and the labor movement itself was such a new imperative; on the other hand, because, with their commitment to fixed principles and defined interests, they are always in danger of confining themselves within a closed camp. In this sense, the political moralism currently raging all over the world is the most guileful form of political blindness because it thinks that being able to be happy with yourself is what it means to be compatible with the world. Of course, these considerations are aimed not at an immoral short-circuit between a hopeless world and unscrupulous souls, but at the medial fixing of moved consciences in the self-regulation of the world. Even so, we have to conceive of the world as an intelligent and generous process which – who knows how – has the opportunity to mean well with itself. Individual consciences would be the intelligent sensors of a world that can use them to heal itself. To be sure, there is no way to do justice to the phenomenon of life without taking into consideration an ontology of Munchausen syndrome. In the context of this syndrome, which is as astonishing as it is successful, new formations of conscience could be interpreted as the self-rescue agencies of the real. They would be the door to opportunity, so to speak, and danger would open it. The rescuing self-mediation of the world presupposes that the voice of conscience is precisely the voice of danger in which the world (through the medium of alert intelligence) sees itself. Only within this function is it still legitimate to speak of conscience. In all other cases, the moralizing conscientiousness that insists on itself creates a lack of conscience in its purest, most vicious form. The Vatican's stance on issues regarding birth control illustrates how this occurs.

Nowhere else is the interpretation of an ontological self-rescue more magnificently formulated than in the couplet of Hölderlin's "Patmos" hymn: "Where danger threatens/That which saves from it also grows."[7] Frequently quoted and rarely understood, this phrase has become the slogan of a salvation philosophy where the development of redemption is both tangibly and vaguely construed as a quantitative mobilization of counterforces. But the growth of what saves from danger is actually to be understood as a reduction – namely, a reduction of rigid subjectivities' resistance to the urgencies of the world process. What does grow when danger is understood is the subject's willingness to perceive danger's ecstatic and medial qualities. Growth of what saves presupposes the responsiveness of individuals to the as yet unspoken imperatives of danger. This is why an increasing attention to danger is the criterion of a politics that strives for a new kind of credibility for reasons that go beyond reputation. If danger is understood as the moment when new consciences are formed, then conscience is no longer just an instance of remembering general principles in the soul's conversation with itself. In its changed function, conscience is the ear for the urgent. If it merely listened to its own principles, these would be nothing but a cover name for the impenetrability of conscience and the self-gratification of the political conscience carriers. Conscience as ear says nothing – it allows for something to be said to it. There is far too much talk of morality and not enough listening – this is especially true in politics. But to learn how to listen, the actors of political praxis would have to take a step back from the deafening mobilizations that constitute the very catastrophe whose preventative measure they claim to be.

In order to successfully strive for a new kind of credibility, the politician must become the medium of an urgency by which the world process works on consciences by overwhelming, provoking, and shattering them. As far as the embodiment of principles is concerned, the lack of credibility of politics is now its great opportunity.

If political dealings are beginning to seem like a hollow spectacle, it would be a disaster if we plugged these new hollow spaces up with old principles. Very little separates hollowness from being receptivity. Only when the primacy of receptivity also permeates the political world can a politics with an ear towards the inevitable become conceivable. A politics that listens would not be windbagging in the service of interest groups. The medial relationship to the urgent is an ecstasy – in it, individuals constitute of more than just their interests and the world is more than its sorry state of affairs. This presents an intriguing prospect for politicians as well. With a little luck, they could become credible contemporaries if they became the authors and not just the targets of the satire that is sure to be written regardless.

5

PARIS APHORISMS ON RATIONALITY

Philosophes, encore un effort si vous voulez être parisiens!
Jean Maurel, *Victor Hugo, philosophe*[1]

All That is Right

Ratio means calculation, measure, proportion, ration, equivalent. Rationality is the principle of perceiving the things that concern us from the point of view of their proportionality, measurability, and predictability. Rationalism is the dogmatic thesis that the measurable, calculable, conceivable, and thinkable essentially constitutes the real itself. Traditional criticism of rationality is the application of rationality upon itself and the reflection on the possibilities and limits of equivalents and adequacies in cognition, action, and judgment. Radicalized criticism of rationality objects to the excessiveness of measuring, dividing, and computing, as well as the immoderateness of rationalism in the establishment of criteria and measuring ranges.

In each of these versions of the phenomenon *ratio*, the idea of *truth as relation* is at play. It entails the assimilation of thoughts and actions to facts and situations. In order for assimilation to take place, however, dissimilation must have existed beforehand. It is only in a desert of missed marks that we can perceive the oases of convergence. The oasis is a place where things are "right"; it is the privileged place where things that correspond to each other fuse together. Culture is the art of creating oases – places where the cultivation of correspondences is intentionally carried out. Having initially begun as an agricultural culture, it owes its existence to the ability to cultivate fields and soils as the "right" habitats for selected plants. Its secret is the correct correspondence of plants and soils, and the right alignment of the action of sowing and harvesting to the seasons. It was only by way of metaphorical seminars that it later spread through other "fields" – until the Cicerone *cultura animi* emerges from it which is what only then humanists really consider to be culture. Until this "culture as such" materializes as a philosophical way of life, the concepts of the rational, the right, the appropriate, and the corresponding remain scattered into a variety of local practices. The multifaceted economy of small instances of rightness precedes the monoculture of the great truth. But only inconspicuous, unrecorded stories tell of these small economies of the right since they are lost in the seeming ahistoricity of the banal. The truth concepts of everyday life have remained silent in the face of self-evidence; speechless with triviality, the small worlds of pre-metaphysical correspondence are on the margins of philosophical interest.

   Who remembers that an even older truth function exists than that of the agricultural "tilling" of the soil – the "truth" of hunters and shooters, for whom the right is what *hits the mark*? The projectile that finds its goal fulfills this type of rightness, which is one of the most fateful that have appeared in the history of rationality – we forget all too easily that the "mark-hitting" accuracy of modern artillery is more consequential for the history of the world today than any adherence to statements or arrival of predictions. Even so, our language has inconspicuously made note of the connection between the function of truth and the ballistic motif. In addition to what hunters and shooters think is right, as a second Archean age, there is a separate rationality of gatherers and seekers, which occurs only when they find what they "can use." The discovery you can take with you is what is right, according to the act of gathering. Even in this, modernity is mostly just an unconscious explorer of an archaic truth function, because all its countless expeditions of scientific research are a continuation, with modern means, of the gathering and taking home of the right discoveries – except that for us it is no longer so clear what the discoveries will do to us in the comfort of our own home. For they have escaped the small *ratio* of seeking and finding and are destroying the old familiar ways of life. These inventions and this research are sweeping through the world like a spring tide that is itself still devoid of truth.

   In addition to the archaic truth functions of hunter-gatherers – the hitting of the mark and the discovery – the ancient arts and crafts have bequeathed us a wealth of inconspicuous concepts of correspondence that establish rules, rations, and appropriateness within local practices. Thus, there is still a concept of truth of pharmacists, where what is right is what *helps*; a tailor's concept of truth, where what is right is what *fits*; a musician's concept of truth, which is measured by what is *in tune*; a carpenter's concept of truth, where what is right is what *joins together*; a mason's concept of truth, where what is done right is what *stands* and *holds* soundly. In all these fields, people gather experience with sub-truths that are inconspicuously pre-sorted into an equivalence between sentences and circumstances. This inconspicuousness is at the same time a criterion for the soundness and sensation-free consideration of these sectoral truth functions. It is only because they are already recorded and assumed to be vital that the later effort of the intellect to find perceptive evident equivalences to things also becomes plausible and self-evident. The intellectual obligation to say what is right about reality accurately and appropriately subsists from the silent analogy to the manifold ways that the right is proven to be valuable in various equivalent fields. We probably would not know what a wrong statement would be if we did not know what a pair of ill-fitting pants felt like. Some theories are wrong – like some shots that miss their mark – and some assumptions prove to be successful – like shots that hit the bull's eye, like treatments that help and notes that are in tune. In this way, hitting the mark, discoveries, fusions, fittings, effects, harmonies, cohesions are regional variants of corresponding phenomena that become clear to every life as soon as it gets a bit more acquainted with them. With the gentle violence of the self-evident, they tune and orient all the complex functions of the human mind in the fields of theory, praxis, and art. It is only because the diverse cultures of correspondence and adequation had already inconspicuously prepared the ground that the higher truths of science, metaphysics, ethics, religion, and aesthetics were able to build their imposing buildings on it.

Diplomats as Thinkers in Destitute Times

When Hamlet performs a diagnosis of history and says that time is out of joint, we can now hear the truth-theoretical undertone in that sentence. The permanent crisis of modern times shakes our most elementary feelings for what is right and what is wrong. A quake runs through the mute subcontinents of what is in tune, what fits, what hits the mark and it destabilizes the very foundations of all the known ways that something can be right.

What has an effect is no longer true; what is in tune no longer fits; what hits the mark no longer helps; what lasts no longer holds together; and it does not go the way you want it to anymore. If we take a closer look at the matter, we notice that this description of a state of affairs has been "hitting the mark" for centuries, even if the twentieth century makes a special claim on it. Ever since the movements of *Sturm und Drang*, Idealism, and Romanticism, modernity has been dancing the roundel of missing the mark. For just as long now, the activities of philosophy have been grouped around the new discipline of the "critique of reason." It uses its means to respond to the new state of affairs where truth and correctness are no longer what they were ever since modernity unleashed unique kinetic phenomena on earth with the help of technology and driven by the spirit of mobilization – these are phenomena that usher in unknown modes of correspondence and non-correspondence. Whichever image we use to represent the modern kinetics of the world – thinking avalanche or secondary vulcanism – it awakens a radicalized reflection on the conditions of possibility for correctness.

Philosophy in volcanic times inevitably becomes a critique of reason. This, too, is an art that undergoes transformations. Today, it cannot do its job either in a traditionally rationalist way where reason is well founded and self-limited *à la* Kant, or in the style of traditional irrationalism where reason is on trial in the name of feeling, will, faith, etc. In view of current ill feelings, it would be touching to swear by the guiding reason of classical Enlightenment or, conversely, take flight into romantic sermons of wholeness. By way of civilizational volcanism (or our existence as a thinking avalanche), too many things are thrown out of joint, too much has missed the mark, been out of tune and disassembled to hope that treatments from the pharmacies of modernity (of all places) could possibly do any good. Today's critique of reason can only be the research that discovers the grounds of correspondences and non-correspondences. Thus, a radical critique of reason adapts itself to an object that has become uncanny.

If nothing is in tune and nothing fits, if nothing hits the mark and nothing helps, then the time has come for diplomats. Their job is to do something in situations where there is nothing left to do. (In this way, they are, incidentally, the descendants of the priests.) As technicians of secondary negotiation, they provide a fine print of truth that matches the harsh modern landscape. For professional purposes, they count on the need for the agreed upon to be considered true. Without being plagued by metaphysical scruples, they indulge a secondary notion of truth and correctness that no longer allows itself to agree on what would be primarily and essentially the thing that fits/works/hits the mark/corresponds.

Partly out of wisdom and partly out of resignation, the philosophy of diplomats is limited to the minimal coordination of dissonant voices and to a loose assembling of what does not correspond as part of a specific interest to get to an agreement. This secondary concept of the truth of diplomats corresponds to the distinctive emergence of a secondary philosophy that has been unmistakable for generations – one that no longer teaches perspectives on life, but has built its operations around current intellectual secondary virtues such as clarity, overview of material, and communicability. Others think that this is a sign that philosophy has recently grown up and abandoned the juvenile vice of thinking about deep questions. And, indeed, philosophers now go to the office in the morning like other officials; they've learned how to manage problems that can't be solved as politely, pragmatically, attentively, and ironically as adults and diplomats are supposed to behave. In fact, the idea of diplomatic unification (with its deliberate understanding of things that it is neither desirable nor enforceable to agree upon) is recommended as a very grown-up practical procedural principle. It replaces convictions with manners – the only case where the term "civilizing process" really fits – and it would be even more likable if it refrained from being right on a grand scale and behaving transcendental-diplomatically as a doctrine empowered by truth. After all, the concept of consensus does not need to advertise its validity with great effort; it could quietly lower its theoretical budget and concentrate on diplomatic craft. If it fails to do so, the suspicion arises that the secondary philosophy is not free from being jealous of the overthrown *prima philosophia*; perhaps it is even homesick for the era of the last established cathedrals. After all, as long as the truth diplomats make lavish efforts towards theory themselves, philosophy as an institution is neither dead nor repealed. It stays alive as long as it surpasses itself. The new division of its business into outbidding activities and diplomatic tasks is the testimony of an unbroken vitality – whereby vitality is to be understood as an ambiguous compliment and wholeness almost as a reproach.

Low Theory

A modern poet who is currently suffering a severe decline in popularity because his left-wing populist overtones do not overlap with today's tastes offers up a memorable consideration:

By nature I have no ability for metaphysics: to think about everything under the sun and how concepts come together with each other is all Greek to me. So I hold to the way of philosophizing which is mainly circulated in the lower classes, what people mean when they say, "Go to that one there for advice, he is a philosopher" or, "That one there can draw some distinctions." When the common people attribute a philosophical attitude to someone, it is almost always an ability to endure something. In a fistfight one distinguishes fighters who are good at taking it and fighters who are good at dishing it out, that is, those who can endure a lot and those who can punch well; and the people understand philosophers, in this sense, as those who can take it; whatever the situation may be. In the following, however, I understand philosophizing as the art of taking it *and* dishing it out in battle (but otherwise, as I said, to remain in general agreement with the people in what philosophizing is supposed to mean).[2]

Rarely does someone act so innocently while giving out insights of such consequence. Brecht's entire break with what he calls metaphysics took place in gesture and skipped over argumentation in a profound and popular way. He apologizes for his inability to conceptualize in order to gain the space for another kind of knowledge. With an easy-to-understand, proletarian cleverness, he uses his lack of understanding as the requirement for a better understanding. Because we can always be sure that Brecht is not speaking from a place of modesty, we can freely admire his populist cold-bloodedness. The man knows that the world is at war; military units are being deployed everywhere, even in the great theories. Filled with mad hope that his self-preservation between the front lines may also have something to do with truth, he evades the maneuvers of logical Gigantomachy. Like Schwejk, he creates himself out of the dust that rises up when the heroes begin to march. He lets the athletes of reflection let their abilities run riot on the argumentation front and concedes to the metaphysicians their exhausting privilege to take up ever more intricate positions in ever more indecisive struggles with ever greater effort. Is he really just prevented by inability, or has he also been tipped off by an insight? He seems to rely on the possibility that a small admission of incompetence sometimes yields as much as the utmost use of great aptitudes. Those who learn about effort through ordinary life experience do understand one thing about philosophy, even if it otherwise remains obscure or irrelevant to them – philosophy comes from effort and leads to effort. In this way, the standoff that is easily perceptible from the outside and hangs over the great metaphysical alternatives can be congenial with the lack of competence for such things. What is free of charge discovers commonality with the most expensive things if it is bold enough to trace the effort of ideas back to the idea of effort. This is low theory's chance. It can rise to Brecht's heights if it grasps that a senseless effort can only be avoided by a timely inability to execute it. It is part of a popular lifestyle to not fall for one's own talents. Inability is a special art. If metaphysics is the heroic effort to lift the weight of the world with the power of theory, then the lack of talent for it is not just the avoidance of a justified demand. Oh, the philosophical Schwejk knows very well that he's been carrying the weight of the world for a long time in his own way, and that he did not have to wait for the effort sermon of the theory capuchins to attain a concept of heaviness.

La chose la mieux partagée du monde

Let us leave the Brechtian Young Hegelianism to rest – together with its eternally bad conscience for never proceeding far enough from theory to praxis. Let us also look past the mannerism of its New Objectivity pugilist morality, with which the sultry nineteenth century transitioned into the cool twentieth. What does make us pay attention is Brecht's legitimate concern about remaining in agreement with the people about the purpose of philosophizing. Here, the essential thing is not the populist gesture. What matters is a downward movement of thought, dressed in metropolitan-populist clothes. (It also existed in the ethnic costumes that have long since seemed silly to us.) The way down – this motif is completely inseparable from the impulses of post-metaphysical philosophy in modernity. Abiding by the abject, seeing the world in a perspective from below, anchoring in the banal – thus and similarly do the guiding programs of a thinking that engages in the mundane resound in order to finally grasp the realness of reality in a non-metaphysical way. However, the great rush of philosophy towards everyday life is the opposite of bending the knee before bon sens, which was once claimed to be the most fairly distributed thing in the world.[3] By lifting the banal philosophically to a higher level, it proves to common sense that it does it no good to be so well distributed. For common sense, everyday life remains a prison from which every life that has not resigned itself to it nevertheless dreams itself free. Philosophy, on the other hand, wants to break out of its empty rooms and into the post-metaphysical fullness of human life, and the mundane is thus the promised land of the tangible. There, people can be found as they are – you surprise them in the middle of work (ah, self-generation of the species), during sexual activity, while with children and in kitchens, and even in the application of rules of linguistic understanding and in convivial self-indulgence – weird and wonderful creatures who make full use of their provisions with sets of everyday knowledge. Intoxicated by these discoveries, metaphysics-weary thinking plunges into the depths, which compensate it abundantly for its loss of idealized height. A hermeneutic of the banal blossoms out of these newly discovered depths, explaining to us what an amazing mystery it is if we make the effort to be there.

But the depths themselves know next to nothing of having been discovered by philosophy, and one can be sure that they would not think much of it if they knew. This is what the poet Brecht so surely encounters in his picaresque indifference to philosophical professionalism. He thinks "like the people" because he aims at a point where we are done with philosophical understanding – with "giddy head and light hands," as our colleague Hofmannsthal says.[4] At the point where the depths have their lowest level and center of gravity, the weight of the world presses down on the individual, and would crush them if they had not learned how to squeeze out from under unbearable weights. By understanding the depths, the mind also understands the burdening nature of reality. One is a philosopher there, where one can endure something. What counts here is "knowledge" as an act of persevering and endurance as a form of understanding. The banal wisdom of the low sees life from the very outset as a nexus of burdens, a web of effort and discomfort. (One does not dare talk about being-in-the-world here; it would sound too luxurious.) But that is not to say that conscious life first takes blows and carries burdens and in addition possesses an idea of the world as burden and a blow. Rather, the world is made available to us to the extent that it has "made us understand" its weight. In the extremely rudimentary knowledge of everyday life, which in itself is not easy to bear, the development of the real is directly fused with the experience and the understanding of heaviness. That is why the "people" identify philosophers as the takers. The takers are the hermeneuticists of heaviness. When the world "clears" in front of them, it always approaches them as a burden that rests on the shoulders of an ability to understand and endure.

Does philosophy now suffer from an Atlas complex? Does it continue its ambition of understanding everything under the auspices of carrying everything? The brave soldier Schwejk shakes his head wearily. He immediately declares his incompetence as soon as the metaphysical Atlas game is to be played with the world. No ambition, no talent, no time. Like all people who handle heavy weights as part of their job, he relies on a technique of tilt where one rolls the loads diagonally and essentially lets them carry themselves. It does not relieve the strain entirely, but it shows us a way to put the burden into the least strenuous relationship with the ground. The effort that remains is still in the top margin of what we must cope with, but without being crushed. The regression into the commonplace reaches its destination with these old stonemasons; what is right is what can still be moved. In everyday life, however, everyone knows that the real bearer of the weight of the world is the ground and not the strained human. The gravity of the commonplace sets limits to the wantonness of theory – even if it may always dream of heroic weightlifting that does not let the great burdens of reality rest on the anonymous ground, but places them on the grounds that oppose the world from within the subject. As long as philosophical thinking exists, it also knows the temptation to deal with the weight of the world in a frivolous way. There is a weightlifter in every thinker.

For athletic thinkers, however, the way down is not without pitfalls. They are overqualified for the simple and too highly trained for the obvious. Such incomparable minds as Brecht and Heidegger have this in common. Neither the lyricist with a penchant for boxing matches nor the masterful thinker from the Black Forest can escape the temptation to extol the way down as a climb towards the thing itself. Although not as paved with heroic trivialism as with the early Heidegger, no one will be able to deny that a gestural commonality exists between Brecht's poetic exploration of the hard, cold, bad, and heavy and Heidegger's existential-ontological elaboration of the idea of a natural world-concept of the commonplace. Both tread on a post-metaphysical terrain in the broadest sense, where the spirit must befriend its finiteness and corporeality. Yet both are ontologically playing the strong man game, and both are enchanted by their own power: Brecht with his boxer's morality, which considers giving to be more blessed than taking, Heidegger with his determined vehemence to hermeneutically control even the inaccessible. Both make it clear to posterity what kinds of risks hem the way down – and what opportunities there are to ridicule oneself with a decisive acceptance of the obvious. But maybe it cannot be any different. Perhaps the hermeneutics of banality must succumb to the temptation of dealing with the task of ordinary life in the style of a weightlifter. Perhaps it is true that the discovery of the obvious is really the most grave for us, and perhaps we really do have to engage in the undertaking to exorcize the metaphysical devil using the post-metaphysical Beelzebub. Well then, philosophers – another endeavor for you should you wish to indulge! We will extol the descent as a high-altitude ascent, we will sell bottled water to the river and tirelessly defend the thesis that nothing is as incomprehensible as the obvious. In this way, perhaps a light astonishment at the burdensome life will one day become the most fairly distributed thing in the world.

Geometry as Finesse

Following tradition, relationships that are called reasonable are those that can claim the "blessing of rightness" or proportionality for themselves. These include: adapting means to ends; coordination of instruments to circumstances; orientation of research towards goals; calculation of expenditures with respect to returns; obligation of statements towards what holds true; the development of theses from premises; ordering the focus of expectations towards the expectations of expectations; the mutual recognition of humans as subjects of reasonable abilities ... with each variation of the principle of reasonableness, new spheres of rightness, justification, appropriateness, harmoniousness, and calculability are accentuated in the cosmos of logic.

But thus far as reasonable thinking becomes aware of itself and feels how astonishing its own emergence from the whole is, it urges itself to say what it has to do with this whole. Hence, philosophy begins with a human enterprise that is more demanding than the construction of pyramids, the installation of irrigation cultures, and the surveying of fields: with the task of presenting the unpresentable and measuring the immeasurable. The philosophical minds of the classical age of metaphysics were geometricians of the immeasurable. Should anything be true of the rumors that speak of the dawn of a post-metaphysical era, then perhaps it is that the failure of the projects to geometricize the disproportionate is impossible to keep secret. They made use of an ontological feint that has become unrepeatable to us: they assumed a proportionality or correctness in the totality of the proportions themselves. The whole is thought of as a circle with geometric finesse; in more modern terms, as a system – and from there it was only a small feat to "rediscover" the intelligible shape of the circle or the system as a whole. This finesse has been unrepeatable since we have known that although phenomena such as the circle and the system occur, it does not mean that the whole is therefore circular or systemic – not even a circle of circles or a system of systems but a turbulence, a fluctuation, a catastrophe, which does not relate to anything but its own singularity. This is why the measuring of the immeasurable ends with fear and trembling. The rulers that reason uses to measure its proprieties do not just have a stake in the intelligible forms, the ideas; they are also participants in the disasters that this singular existence has directed onto its unpredictable trajectory. Within the light of reason, there also shines the natural light of catastrophe that advances through us.

Unconcealment and Tolerability

As we know, Heidegger tirelessly insisted on the revelation that the Greek word for truth, *aletheia*, was composed of the word for the dark, hidden, forgotten, *lethe*, and its negation. The philosophical genius of the Greeks became apparent to him from this inconspicuous fact. If the ordinary vocabulary of a people defines truth as the negative of hiddenness and forgetting, we are dealing with a language that effortlessly thinks the most profound thoughts. Heidegger thought that he could expect as much of German, and translated the Greek *aletheia* with the term "unconcealment" (*Unverborgenheit*). (Although the Humboldtian translation of the word as "overtness" was philologically slightly more correct, it was philosophically significantly inferior.) If unconcealment belongs to the truth, then its fate falls together with the event through which it becomes unconcealed – with disclosure, arising, revelation (and the opposite event that leads to forgetting and a second concealment). The disclosing revelation through which all that is rational and proportionate is laid open is itself neither rational nor proportionate. The "space" of the true as the unconcealed pops up singularly like an island full of commensurable conditions from an ocean of incommensurability and disproportion. Where humans are, that's where the forefield of the covertly monstrous can also be found. Their cultures populate a zone that is both paradise and volcano – an ontological Hawaiian and Lanzarote effect. With his term "clearing" (*Lichtung*), Heidegger, the hesitant heir of European light metaphysics, has reminded us of the eventful rise of a graspable space for proportionalities. Because he not only sees the visible in the clearing, but also visibility, he understands himself not as an Enlightener, but as a seer. While the Enlightener practices a phosphoric light-making praxis and uses light as a tool for illuminating the substance, the seer lingers in the "deeds and sufferings of light." Imagining is not seeing. For the one who really sees, the eye is an ear of light.

What would Brecht the Enlightener have to say about Heidegger the seer? He would probably make a small distinction. "So far," he would say, "everything is very simple, even if metaphysical terms are all Greek to someone like me. But even a child gets it that what the seer does here corresponds precisely to what takers do in boxing. The seer is a philosopher because he endures something, and he endures something because he is a real man and, besides, it comes from his position. I, however, would like to from now on recognize under seeing both taking *and* giving in a boxing match. Otherwise, though, as I said, I want to remain in agreement with those who endure something."

For the taker, unconcealment does not mean visibility, but tolerability. For what is to be taken at all moves in the range between what is quite easy to do and what cuts unbearably deep. It's not so much the limits of illumination and visibility that separate the concealed from the unconcealed, but stress limits, pain limits, tolerability limits. It is not what one has heard or read about the world that decides one's understanding of the world, but what one has gone through and endured from it. If one admits that philosophy, as soon as it is dealing with the whole, speaks only in serious puns anyway, then at the critical point one would have to talk not about the clearing, but about the direction. The projects of culture and enlightenment are less about the spread of light and more about the overpowering of burdens. Ever since humans have felt the will to know, they have been interested not so much in elucidation as in alleviation – and it is only because there are elucidations that are also alleviations (or lead to alleviations) that intellect and insight are so popular.

A metaphysical determination of the playing field of all analogies where truths can become apparent to us leads to the original liaison between the recognizable and the tolerable – the lucid and the easy. For endurance is the most authoritative of all ratios to emerge to us out of the disproportionate and intolerable. What should exist for us exists in the realm of the tolerable or not at all. In this sense, all philosophy is algosophy – measurement of the fields of tolerances that are possible for us. Only the moderately heavy, the portable, even the light has the prospect of being incorporated into the corpus of an enduring understanding. From the unbearable, the over-heavy, the exalted, one can only know as much as remains in the traces of remembrance when one has survived it. Perhaps some theologies speak of precisely this when they say that the space for man was opened only by the retreat of God. Only indirect signs remain in our consciousness of the presence of the super-powerful, of the exaggerations, flashes, ecstasies, breakdowns; only footsteps of the heavyweights that limit and warn us. No idea includes the measured in itself, and just as the eye cannot fix the sun or death, so no knowledge holds on to the disproportionate, hardly even finds a name for it – chaos, hell, primal pain, sacred, sublime, being, nothingness, Dionysus, Shiva. What we know as rationality is a way to deal with the "real," which only becomes possible through the mind's original and unmissable evasion of the incommensurable powers, a way of coping that turns towards the bearable, imaginable, well established, agreeable. The agreeable originated in our necessary skirting of the unavoidable. This evasion as a dodging of the overly heavy is the basic effort around which all subjectivities are grouped. Subjectivity can only be lived as the self-imposed effort to remain within the sphere of the tolerable. It recognizes itself in its efforts to preserve itself, and if it lost that effort, it would no longer be subjectivity, but the all-encompassing unity of everything within an utterly alleviated consciousness. That is why pure theory is the ultimate luxury – something for dandies and suicides. Only they have access to the mystery of frivolity – for the alleviation of life until the annihilation of burdens.

Ordinary mortals find life difficult. They remain condemned to the effort to alleviate their burdens to the best of their ability. But the dream of burdenless ease is alive in them, too. They tirelessly strain to make it easier for themselves. Through their combined efforts, the process of civilization becomes an undertaking that brings about involuntary enlightenment. The enlightenment efforts of culture have themselves become the intolerable burden which they were supposed to evade by moving towards the tolerable.

Of the Foolishness to Not be an Animal

But how much does the human being who measures everything, in turn, measure up to the world in which they exist? How does the ontological animal fit into the totality of the other beings? How do beings with the ability to notice coherences cohere with their world? How does the subject who assimilates things with their engineering skills become assimilated to what was there before? How does the being who is gifted with an insight into circumstances fit into the context of all circumstances?

To ask in this way is to reveal the answer in the questions. The human being is the entity who does not fit. Their relationship to relations is disproportionate. It is right for them to not be quite right.

It should not be difficult for anyone who knows the material to hear in these formulations an echo of Nietzsche's and Heidegger's forays to explore the truth about truth. Both have the common insight that humans do not enter the space of truth like actors on an already finished stage, but that they themselves are the stage above which the strangest light appears: knowledge. Being a stage is the possibility of having a relationship to relations. This second relationship contains the mystery of the "truth as such," beyond local correctness. The adventure of not being natural is located in it. The relationship to relations is apparent when humans' horizontal interwovenness tears into the fabric of the world so that the vertical is revealed with its double meaning of high/deep. This dimension witnesses the human exodus from biology, the subject's resignation from symbioses, and humans' discovery that they do not fit, that they have become disproportionate. As far as they are the disproportionate beings who drop out of their environment in natal precarity, humans become susceptible to the truth question. The sacred word "truth" – which is more ridiculous than anything ordinary as all exalted things are – recalls the promises given to our lives: that the fallen-out being is capable of being included; that the disproportionate exists within proportion; that even the independent can depend on something; that loneliness has a counterpart; that even the unbound can be bound together with something. The question of truth presented us with a bill for the luxury of becoming human. The essence of truth is the foolishness to not be an animal.

Invent Yourself!

High cultures reach their critical phase when individuals are no longer limited by something external to them – when there is no "tutelary nature" to oversee their life-functions. From that point on, self-knowledge becomes a significant topic of the art of life. The view inward is supposed to discover systems that compensate for the loss of earlier synchronies between human and nature. From then on, the hope of reason rests on an "inner law" that provides the right guidance for human beings after their outward separation and isolation. But that hope is deceptive. Those who seek to find order by taking the path towards an interior that no longer has a foothold on the outside become victims of an irony. (One could also say that they become mystics, provided that mystics are the victims of an irony who then agree to the sacrifice and merge with the ironic.)

This irony belies the hope for order with its own driving force. If reasonable subjects reasonably explore themselves, they ultimately discover not regulative variables but an energetic abyss. Recognizing oneself means not determining an identity, but becoming aware of a disproportionality.

If someone was to believe that the path inward attests to a secret image of the self, they would be proven wrong through self-knowledge.

What remains of the pathos of reason that should have told us what we are? The imperative of wisdom "Know thyself!" transforms into the existential motto "Be yourself!" This is a cavalier ontological motto that allows every relative to be whatever they wish if they just think that being means being from the best family. In the small village of being, this is the local rightness that gives human behavior a benchmark. But aside from its uplifting effect, the phrase "Be yourself!" is a bit too weak for practical guidance in this area. The cavalier concept of reasonableness does not yet help one get through the adventurous daily routine. Then the advice goes on to say that to be yourself, you must also help yourself and let others help you. From here, we are not too far away from a paramedic concept of reason as first aid, where what is right is that which counters the urgent first. This corresponds most closely to the accidental nature of historical life. But existence consists not only of its accidents but also of its successes. Be yourself thus means "Invent yourself!" This is answered by the poetic concept of reason where what is right is what agrees to the unique opportunity of life. As René Char says: "Only one perk is given to us together with death: to create art before it comes" (*"Nous n'avons qu'une ressource avec la mort: faire de l'art avant elle"*).[5]

6

AFTER MODERNITY

HAMM [*anguished*]: What's happening, what's happening?
CLOV: Something is taking its course.

Samuel Beckett, Endgame[1]

The Age of the Epilogue

In recent times, the prefix "after" has made a noteworthy career for itself. Hardly any article or feature supplement would be considered up to date without it. In the form of the Latin "post," more recent cultural criticism is speckled with it; it emits a flair of elegant reflexivity; it suggests that something is happening because something else is over; its property includes a consciousness that has seen many worlds come and go, including those that wanted to become a beautiful new one. Used correctly, the prefix pushes the past away as if it were a position that has become untenable. In one sentence, it jumps into a present that can always claim to come after the past. We do not know much of this past, and yet it is a unique feeling to have it be behind us. A small "after" and world ages become outdated. Post-modernity – it has a strange ring to it. Never before did someone give such a cold goodbye to yesterday. With just one prefix, you are ahead of your epoch. What does this tell us?

The career of the prefix "after" suggests that although shocking things happen, we no longer have a conception of history at our disposal that would allow the present to date itself. Since the general impression that history has no road map is spreading, we feel our way forward through a processual no man's land. The unleashed realities seem to be neither communicable nor predictable – never mind the idea of subsuming them under a historico-philosophical schema. And no specific epoch name seems to fit the present either; we can't even clearly distinguish epochs and trends. You might get the impression that the matter of reality is itself changing and evaporating into something unimaginable.

For this reason, post-modernity cannot be the term for an epoch with any kind of claim to historico-philosophical materiality, but only an index for increases in reflection. But what increases with this reflection is only the sobering effect of contemplation and nothing more. Post-modern reflexivity does not lead to peaks where a self-made and self-satisfied consciousness can look down onto its age, having made the climb. Expansive views, cross-sections, panoramas – who wouldn't like them, and with them the ecstasy of the broad context, the summit experience that can capture its age in thought? But when thinking goes about its task today, it is not in the mood for summit expeditions – it remains completely post-conceptual and post-culminating, it abstains from the old ascension fantasies that would have us characterize the processes in social and logical reality with progressive-alpine metaphors. Process and progress only have a deceptive rhyme in common, and post-modernity does not set much in store for it. Sure, we continue to advance, but not upward – that is the quintessence of post-progressive reflections on the relationship between mind and time – and this confirms that pre-modern spirits are also to be found in the post-modern hustle and bustle for whom the wheel of fortune makes far more sense as a symbol for historic time than a ladder of progress. Those who live later do not know better – this fact marks the end of the historical experiment that wanted to force the truth to increasingly "stand out" over time. What has really emerged in the course of the experiment is precisely that it is by no means certain that a later knowledge is the better one.

Post-modern feelings of process are not those of people that believe that they are going uphill historically. They are more likely to be the sensations of passers-by on an escalator where you make automatic progress, whether you abide by the rule to stand to the right or to walk to the left. As long as you are on the escalator, it constantly proceeds forward in one direction – but comparing an escalator with the idea of progress would be an overinterpretation, to say the least. The spatial and kinetic metaphors of the Old Enlightenment no longer belong here, and the concept of ascension is also unsuitable for marking location differences on escalators. If one rolls down, the other rolls further up; the distance between the two has no evolutionary purpose and cannot translate into a leading edge for the top-rolling one, even if it seems to be the one that has gotten "further" – further to the "height of the age," whose high position amounts to being here and now, and nothing else.

Ever since progress has become automatic, optimism about the future has transformed into process melancholy. We are no longer driving out of Genoa into modernity; we are rolling on a conveyor belt into the unpredictable. Our own movement hardly counts compared to the total bulk of movement, and the steps that the individual can take on their section of the escalator disappear almost without trace in the rolling whole. Furthermore, although no one knows where the escalator leads, it's hard to suppress the thought that even the longest conveyor belt must eventually end and throw its passengers off.

Since all this has become entrenched into a modern "order of things," briefings on the escalator have become a mass necessity. One has to fear that today's cultural enterprise is no longer much more than the sum of the intellectual hobbies of escalator riders. Even these hobbies are now so imbued with their own automatism that it makes little difference whether someone moves affirmatively or critically on this escalator – indeed, one can even move revolutionarily. There has been no effective difference between the movement of the escalator and the cultural manifestations on it for a long time now, because the field of culture as a market of differences is itself entirely organized like an escalator. Through its motor activity, the things of yesterday are constantly de-actualized; from the gesture of de-actualization itself, a new actuality is launched and already overthrown in its design stage, one volatility chasing the other.

The gesture that corresponds to continuous operations is that of the obituary. It is the dominant form of expression of a culture that lives entirely on the game of current de-actualization; for this reason, the "post" of post-modernism primarily means the "after" of obituary. No form of speech is as adequate to the principle of escalator culture as the obituary, which, in the midst of permanent movement and chronic ambiguity, recalls the last sure fact: the past is not the present. In a time and place where no one can know what will happen tomorrow, it seems almost like a gift that at least the past is over. It thereby provides a criterion that weathers storms. Contemporary culture is a large machine that emits epilogues and creates a hint of orientation in the present by suspending the past. Contemporary brains are at the moment still warm from the iteration of the last epilogic surges – this entire post-Freudian, post-Marxist, post-structuralist, post-metaphysical rhetoric, with which the respective speakers appeared to be at the highest level of possibility for fifteen minutes. The more violent the defamation of the past, the sooner a space for new settlements opens up in the present, even if it is only an illusion of space. For the citizens of escalators, only the epilogic overtaking of the latest trend can achieve the coveted contemporary ecstasy, without which no modern generation can stand itself. As if under duress, the glance falls backwards – by no means forwards, where the journey of the conveyor belt would show that it leads into hopelessness. We prefer to have modernity behind us rather than the eternity of the escalator in front; to cavort in the post-modern rather than in the purgatory of a unitary civilization; to stand at the open grave of the age of progress than before that turn into the future that economic advisors want to talk us into. For contemporary consciousness, death no longer means the "impossibility of having a project," as Levinas once put it, but the impossibility of giving an excuse. It may be that we do not take it far with such speeches, but with its epilogic genius, the much-maligned post-modernism reaches an optimum of the presently possible mental states in spite of everything. For this is just the way it is – every incoherent dreamer creates programs, but epilogues require a modicum of awareness and a sense of context.

Additionally, the "after" comes from the after of after-school detention,[2] where we only too often have to stay to make up the missed lessons of modernity. There are reasons to believe that for a large majority of contemporaries, a substantial modernity has not yet occurred, and that it could only arrive in the form of making up and reviewing. Moreover, a lot of suspect figures can be seen spooking around at the moment, wanting to skip a grade directly into post-modernism from the bushes or the Biedermeier, without getting to know even a little bit of modernity in-between. They will show whether post-modern times might have enough class and forming power to make the new bushmen sit down for detention.

The "after" of after modernism has yet another meaning that extends past that of the epilogue and the obituary. The obituary and the declaration of the death of yesterday are not enough. At least within a dark corner of their consciousness, everyone knows that the automatism of the world process conceals perspectives other than just the "and so on" of the obedient escalator. There is also something catastrophic and unparalleled with which the escalator only has automatism in common, but otherwise propels us forward with a completely different type of movement. We are subjective elements, plugged into a historico-planetary chain reaction that we called "history" in its relatively slow phase and which now seems to be running right to the point of explosion. What we would have to say in view of such threatening things does not seem to be an epilogue, but a prognosis, because we are talking about a catastrophe that has been going on for a long time whose biggest blows are yet to come. In truth, this prognosis is the most radical form of eulogy – namely, a prophetic epilogic that obits to us from a location after annihilation, letting us know what will be said about us then. Thus, the current epilogic apocalyptic breaks through the wall of time and, as if from the other side of fate, talks about the events on this side of the wall. This results not only in an anticipatory epilogue on humanity, but also in the very strange sense that the speakers must think of themselves as dead in order to take the point of view from which they will tell the truth. The "after" of post-modernism reveals itself here as the "after" of self-indulgence with which a civilization convinced of its untenability gives itself an account of its prospects. The Enlightenment is completed in the coincidence of prognosis and obituary, culminating in an absolute necrology that overtakes every possible future and now already pronounces doom as the last word of knowledge. That is why the present, which examines its future perspective, is forced to speak of itself in a tragic future tense and deliver its own eulogies ahead of time because there will be no other speakers to do it in due course. Aren't most animal films today already obituaries to animals, eulogies for entire species? Does anthropology thus turn into a zoology of the necrological animal?

This is where an unforeseen "after" comes into play. It belongs to an awareness that has the aforementioned self-eulogies behind it – at least in the sense that it has heard and understood them and yet cannot stop there. Obviously, even the most routine pessimism is limited to the fact that bad predictions travel faster than bad events. Before they arrive, the observation that we still exist, in spite of everything, remains true. Even premature obituaries do not change the fact that new days are dawning until further notice, as fragile and temporary as all previous ones. The waking spirit sometimes survives the red-hot despair at its own finiteness. Set against a background of downfalls, our stay in the temporary act of the real starts to become strangely cheerful – the worries translucent, the uncertainties self-confident. Perhaps adulthood was never anything other than an encrypted word for what comes after despair. We are still breathing, the sun is still rising, we still learn the most important thing from the day in the main news. The last days are still hidden, the Apocalypse is being put on the shelf for now to join the other unsightly literature, the black tailcoat for humanity's funeral stays in the closet, the Eschaton shows patience. This post-desperate life resembles carelessness to a tee and differs from blindness only in barely noticeable details. We say post-modernism with a misunderstood smile, as if we knew that it should be called still-modernism.

If we were to characterize the specific time structure of contemporary life, we would come up with the concept of an interim that is *after* the prognosis of the worst and *before* the verification of the predictions by the actual. There is no more appropriate term for such a situation than that of the interim.[3] However, our interim does not have a precise deadline, but leaves the day, hour, and cause of the disaster open. Because of this, life, too, can set itself up and spread out within the extended interim as if it were safe. It is only in the ambiguity of the interim that hope finds its playing field. That is why hope is not a principle, but a secondary product of uncertainty about the bad outcome of history. While hope has become effective as a history-making force, its effects are borrowed from eschatology and the inaccuracy of our knowledge about the limits of the interim. This explains why the word "hope" must not be writ large either now or in the future. Its real place is behind the scenes and its appropriate key is *pianissimo*. Only Bloch was allowed to raise his voice on the subject of hope because, unbeknownst to him, he wrote its obituary – the only legitimate occasion to transfigure an effect into a principle. Moreover, loud talk about hope is nowadays just cynical fabrication. Those who want to wage aggressive hope campaigns belong in the neighborhood of the leading German columnist who is supposed to have said after Chernobyl: "Life is distasteful. It just keeps going." The same can be said of the hope that is rightly claimed to belong to life. The only thing that helps hope in its macabre alliance with this obstinately continuing life is unyielding discretion. In the future, we must place private hopes under confessional secrecy and threaten prison sentences for public hope. Those who actually have hopes should bury them as deep as they can – for they can only be helpful as silent forces. Only as such do they not get mixed up with those series of causes that lead to catastrophe. This is the only way in which they do not contribute to the mobilization of enterprises against one's better judgment. Only thus will they become forces of life, doing their work behind individuals' backs and carrying them over the abysses above which the worlds of daylight have been erected.

The Interim – or: The Birth of History from the Spirit of Postponement

The term "interim" not only describes the playing field shared by illusion and hope; it is also reminiscent of the basic shape of Western historical thinking. For what history means in the eminent occidental sense of the word can only be understood from its nature as time limit and interim. An interim can only exist where an event in time strives for a final goal or a final date from which it can be understood as a deadline. These are precisely the basic features of the late Jewish and Christian perception of history, which is constitutive of Europe as a phenomenon. Few historians have fully conveyed how a large swath of history has been shaped by the tradition and variation of messianic and eschatological motifs – not only early Western history, but also modern times, including the recent present. But as for the program of a critique of historical reason, which has been open since Mar and Dilthey, there should be no doubt that messianology, as it emerged from the Jewish tradition and made history in its Christian variant, must form its core.

The messianic perception of history is based on the idea that the long march of peoples through the deserts of time must one day come to an end – when the Messiah completes the alienation era and establishes a final kingdom that does not resemble the current world in any way whatsoever. The Christian version of this model became effective at the moment when Jesus accepted the insinuation of his disciples that he was the Messiah and began to preach the presence of the kingdom of God within him. (The two most revealing variants of such a process are provided by Sabbatai Zwi in the seventeenth and Jiddu Krishnamurti in the twentieth century.) After the disaster of Golgotha, it became clear what explosive power lay in this process. The possibility of Christian messianism was laid out in the unbearable paradox that the Messiah did not prevail as a world king of end-times, but left the scene as a miserable executed criminal. For the first believers, this scandal could only be surmounted with the proclamation of an imminent return of the Lord in all his glory – visible to all, liberating for the faithful, appalling to adversaries. Thus, at the beginning of the Christian concept of history, world time is transformed into a waiting period, which shrinks the horizon to the small span between the crucifixion and the reappearance of the Messiah. It is from this minimum that the later expansions of the horizon had to emanate, and they were due once the waiting for a return became existentially impossible. The first generation of Christians died with a question to which European history would be the answer: How is the absence of the Messiah to be understood? The very next generation had to learn to expect greater time spans and move the Parousia to the time of their grandchildren or great-grandchildren. For them, the question of a Christian's involvement in the business of this world became pressing – and if not with body and soul, nevertheless with great obligation as it would be commanded if tomorrow the last judgment came and the final kingdom began. It was in the musings of the early Christians that Western history was put on its very strange trajectory. Back then, patience and hope first entered into a historicizing tension with each other. Never before had hope been so elevated to virtue and aggrandized into religious psycho-politics. It may be said that the Christian revolution set in motion by Paul intervened more deeply in the experience of time in the Old World than any reform of the imperial calendar could ever have. For Paul, too, the time ahead is a terse interim. But its significance is not that of an inconsequential passage; it is a time with its own dignity insofar as it already stands in the light of salvation by virtue of its message. Consequently, all cosmic and mythical calendars are invalidated.

Even with the caveat of the short interim, existence *post Christum* stands out as an epoch in its own right and is as differentiated from the pre-messianic life of the Jews as it is from the world of the Greeks and Romans. Paul is presumably the first person to live in a hurry as a matter of principle, because it was important to him to fulfill his universally understood mission in the supposedly short period of time given. For him, the content of the mission lies in the revolutionary newness of every life after Christ. The extent to which the epoch-making power of this turning point extends is demonstrated not least by the fact that the present rumors of a *post-modernity* would be groundless without the Pauline *post-antiquity*. Without Paul's great success, there would be no Christianity as world religion, and without that, no periodization of history whose dissolution moves contemporary minds. Christianity as a historical religion, however, stands and falls with the awareness that the time between the crucifixion and the return of the Messiah participates in an epochal newness and thus possesses an objective redemptive-historical content. If this consciousness had not been effective, the Christian impulse would have been lost in the syncretism of late antiquity after a few generations. The non-return of Christ would have drained the expectation of salvation and deprived the Christian message of any future history-making character. A mystical and symbolist psychotherapeutic would probably have absorbed the Christ legend and dissolved it into a self-redemption theory of an Eastern type. The early history of the church, which represents a single struggle against the gnostic temptation of the individual exit from the real history of salvation, shows how powerful the tendencies to such developments were. Only after centuries of wrangling could the real existing church, as a Catholic one, prevail against the private salvation cults and constitute itself as a political organon of salvation and hope for a new world time. The new era is already developed in the fantastic apostolate of the thirteenth Apostle, who felt expressly called to bring the news of Christ to the peoples of the entire non-Jewish world. In Paul's person, that which will become the historical content of the new world age is crystallized for the first time: the self-transcendence of Judaism.

Since then, Christian world time has been substantially an *apostolic time* – time for the spread of an exuberant and counter-worldly message; time for the (however contradictory) installation of justice and fraternity in a desert world; time for the instilling of hope into decaying souls which the war of life had set on a greedy and desperate trajectory. A considerable need for time becomes apparent for this unprecedented mission, as the Christianization of peoples cannot happen overnight. In the light of the missionary idea, the delayed Parousia can be understood not only as a disappointment, but also as a salvation-bringing postponement of the end. If the story really eats from the apostolic substance, then the end of days must not come before the universalization of the message.

Almost from the very beginning, Christian thinking about time and history thus contains the contrast between an eschatological (short) and an apostolic (long) determination of the interim within itself.[4] While the eschatological motif constantly reminds us of the closeness of Judgment Day, the apostolic motif keeps the story open as a time of spreading salvation over the inhabited earth. In the struggle between these two poles, the tense time structure of the Christian world age attains its profile. This is the sign of revolutionary impatience as well as conservative continuity; the élan of messianic unrest as well as the inertia of the sacramental establishment; the eschatological readiness for the end of days as well as the anti-eschatological engagement with the temporary. Where the motif of the long story rules in mature comprehensiveness, there the apostolic goal-orientedness of time emerges most clearly – for it is only from the point of the successful outcome of the mission that the connection to world history as total salvation event can be made visible. With his apostolic program for the post-ancient world, Paul became not only the founder of the Christian religion, but also the initiator of a "sacred mobilization" that has deployed a large part of the psychological and political energy of Europe over the span of millennia.[5]

For the modern phase of the "Christian West," however, it is characteristic that the eschatological element is increasingly pushed into the background. The idea of history as a time between creation and redemption, or between death and Parousia of the Messiah, loses its plausibility in the demarcated horizon of "modern troubled history." "Christian woe" – which no longer even senses its contradiction in terms – begins to arrange itself in a forwardly open continuum. The burdensome thought of a final end is obscured by the philosophy of infinitely perfectible progress. Thus, from the eighteenth century onwards, Christian ideas against traditional Christianity become paradoxically effective by creating decidedly post-Christian or anti-Christian philosophies of history. It is precisely in the decidedly worldly and atheistic wings of the Enlightenment that the messianic impulse, chastened for a millennium, reawakens to radical offensiveness. It becomes world-political violence in Marxism above all and gives a messianic perspective to modern progressive thought – a perspective back onto a beginning from the point of view of an end; the end of the path through the desert of an alienated interim and to the beginning of an era of post-historical fulfillment. It seems that the Christian impulse in modernity reaches a worldly maximum of influence under an atheist, socialist, and humanist incognito. At the same time, it witnesses its irreligious liquidation as well.[6]

The present is indeed a time of historical ambiguity. It is typical for it not to be able to decide between religion and irreligion in the same way it can't decide between the proclamation and revocation of progress. Even though Western civilization has undoubtedly entered a post-Christian age, the departure from the Christian era does not entail a departure from its conception of history and its eschatology. On the contrary, one cannot avoid the impression that the eschatological motif of the Judeo-Christian tradition begins to dominate more forcefully in post-Christian times than ever before. The Judeo-Christian apocalyptic lives on in the neo-pagan panic. The end of the Christian world-epoch does not mean that the apocalyptic stress is followed by a new-cosmological sigh of relief. Only in our grandfathers' generation could we buy into the vision of becoming the new Greeks; up until the eve of National Socialism, it was seductive to think together with Nietzsche that one could emigrate from Christian decadence to pagan health and sacrifice history for the cosmos. Even if, for most contemporaries, Christianity may only be an unreal citable magnitude, no generation has ever been as distant as today's from the cosmic cycle of the times. Never has the return from linear history to a cyclical order of things been as unlikely as it is now. Of course, anyone who is reeling on the sloping trajectory of natural devastation would like to find safety in a cosmological post-history where a sovereign timeless existence prevails. Without a doubt, it would be appealing to settle in a post-Paulinian way and without illusory hope as "tremendous" mortals on the maternal earth. But it is clear that this resettlement is not going to happen, because the world process initiated by Christian hope as well as by the Greek epistemes has gotten disastrously out of control. There is no real pleasure in living. There seems to be no room left in our countdown for the desirable large cosmic cycles.

Chatter about post-modernism bursts into this situation. It drives the dilemma that has been latent for over a hundred years, to the point where it gets out of hand in an open scandal. As soon as a consciousness comes forward that claims to speak of a post-modern location, modernity is lured out of the reserve by this presumption and forced into the confession that it sees itself as the epoch that no other can follow. Post-modern talk, which at first was only meant to provide a bit of variety, forces modernity to profess to be the end of times, that is, an era that no longer wants to have an interim character, but has crossed over into the enduring presence of an infinitely perfect post-history. For modernity, the mere thought of post-modernism is illegitimate and shocking, because according to its self-image, the successors of modernity must never be anything other than modernity, once again.

The dull escalator feeling now proves to be a symptom of historico-philosophical significance: according to its basic historical feature, the present is already a small-scale end of times, which only has itself in front of it. A "post-modern" epoch can no longer be created, except in the bad sense that shocking regressions or catastrophes could destroy the entire construct of the modern age. Because modernity is already a secret millennium burdened with complexes, seen from within it, only the worst can still lead beyond it. This is where we touch on the most anxious point of the contemporary crisis: as long as modernity does not confess that it has established itself discreetly but relentlessly as an end-times kingdom, it remains stuck in its claim that after modernity no other age is permitted to create new epochs. It insists on this claim with an unconscious violence and is plunged into an irresolvable dilemma: on the one hand, modernity can only see the worst as coming after itself; on the other hand, the worst is precisely placed on modernity's own trajectory, which it forbids us to leave because it cannot conceive of a possible alternative to it. It can therefore neither reach nor really even imagine a future for itself. If it continues as before, it produces the worst; if it were to cease producing the worst, it would no longer be itself, but something epochally different. But since it literally sees "nothing" else coming after modernity, it remains condemned to itself. Through its unspoken and uncorrectable belief in itself as the very last era, modernity is fixated on the murky linear processualism that it inhabits, and the only thing it can see ahead is the postponement of the end, but no longer the possibility of something new.

The escalator babble about post-modernism is now becoming expensive. The gallery owners, architects, zeitgeist designers, and cultural editors are losing control of it and it is rising to become a question of epochs in the exact sense of the word – it puts the epochal quality of the present to the test. Thus, the question becomes explicit and undeniable as to whether modernity indeed already has the character of being an end-times or if it is an interim that can be surpassed. In other words, does it still form a section of an open history or rather already the final formation of the occidental-planetary civilizing process? For the busy zeitgeist critics in the media, the problem can also be raised as to whether fashion has already replaced history.

Thus the "after" of after modernity emerges from its cocoon in the last instance as the "after" of a Western age that is still looking for itself. It is an "after" that shakes at the prison-window bars of the present and gives expression to a doomsday claustrophobia. There, the *small talk* of post-modernity is done with and the delicious prefix is just a symptom of panic; it is a powerless postulate that maybe, after the immanent end-times which we know ourselves to be caught in, new spans of time could open themselves for a post-historical human existence. Whoever says the word "post-modernism" just wants to take their neck out of the noose of history. The future prospects of a civilization now hinge on the sense or nonsense of a prefix, and although it was not meant so seriously at first, the involuntary seriousness of the matter has rendered its own reckless origins entirely forgotten. What is at stake here is in fact nothing less than the possibility of a post-modern historicity, in other words, the chance for a post-historical temporality. And yes, such questions do sound like a "betrayal of history." The ominous prefix leads its users into historico-philosophical illegitimacy. It seduces us to play with the unimaginable and makes us willing to travel into a future that no longer constitutes modernity. A small "after" or a tiny "post" and the misty outline of a time beyond the end of history emerges from the realm of what has never been before.

Truth and Symbiosis: On the Geological Sublation of World History

Aristotle said that drama is more philosophical than history; but physics (understood as dialectically transparent) is more philosophical than history and drama combined.

Ernst Bloch, *Experimentum Mundi*[7]

Certainly, it is appropriate to use terms such as "national spirit" and "national character" only with reservations for all time to come. Nevertheless, we cannot deny that there is a "typically German" sensibility for the apocalyptic dimension of history. This sensibility has a theoretical drive and a moral foundation. Whether it is about thousand-year-old empires or the twilight of the gods, messianic tendencies or fears of the end of times, the foundation of invisible churches or utopian communication communities – the German vote on such questions always reveals itself through an unmistakably singular accent that is entirely its own. The strongest conceptual models of historical interpretation through which modernity wanted to come to an understanding of itself are signed by Hegel, Marx, Weber, Bloch, and Habermas, on the one hand, and Nietzsche, Spengler, Heidegger, Taubes, and Löwith, on the other. They can all be distinguished by a logical instinct to characterize the way of the world as a drama of generalization or realization in historical time. As for the moral-political side of the current German end-times sensibility, it gets its seriousness from the memory of the unforgivable twelve years in which the Germans staged themselves as a providential people. German fascism was more than just an impudent grasp for "world domination"; its mythological engine was driven by a racist chiliasm – to use Jacob Taubes's terms, it was driven by a theo-zoology that employed the means of a religious biopolitics to stir up the masses to an unprecedented destructiveness. With its essential gesture, it performed the rebellion against the Judeo-Christian-liberal tradition of Europe; as a war against Judaism, it was an attempt to outbid the status of Jewry as a chosen people through German self-proclamation.

Against such a background, historico-philosophical aspirations are from the outset to be understated. Based on German premises, it would be suspect to have *no* difficulties with the philosophy of history. This does not just mean that the notorious "German spirit" was ripe for an analytical cooling. More important is the fact that a historico-philosophical warning has imprinted itself in the national memory; more precisely, a warning against manically lived historicism and a dread of the violence that can stem from taking historico-religious interpretive models of the world literally. Thinking after 1945 means carrying a millennium on one's back; in this position, no de-Germanization can make a difference. A certain post-millenarian nervousness has been part of the regional character here since the end of the Third Reich. Through all justified and necessary efforts to be a "normal democracy," the German resignation from historico-religious presumption shines through – imperceptibly, but significantly. It is a specialty of post-fascist Germans to consciously *not* be a chosen people any longer. In this way, they present themselves anew as a negative unicum. From their manic historicism, they have retreated into a post-historical modesty; they now practice the powerful melancholy of the day after. They have developed a relationship to the missions of history that resembles that of a sober alcoholic to their former drug. It may be assumed that, until further notice, they will adhere to an experience that lies ahead of those people that are still undertaking missions, still manic, still making history. Through an unprecedented defeat, they have been brought to the unwanted but valid insight that national identities and ethnic missions are in principle nothing more than violent and violence-producing collective autohypnosis. Under its effect, the historical actors rush to the stage, guided by self-insinuations, to conquer their place in the world-historical sun. If we soberly take stock of the infernal adventure of the Germans, we create an ability to see through the dealings of history-making nations that make us shudder: "history" could now be understood as that which results from competing social manias, driven by the real-theatrical competition between autohypnotic imperial collectives, each of whom want to play out their world delirium *to the end* and lead it to supremacy. Even if we do not dare say it out loud, it is one of the psycho-historical peculiarities of post-fascist German intelligence to possess a sensorium for those tendencies that conjure up new life-threatening equations between real-theater and real-politics (to whom it may concern …).[8]

Meanwhile, no one can accuse the Germans of not wanting to learn the Western lesson. As special students of modernism, they have understood that life in the twentieth century can mean nothing more than self-assertion in a "risky and ultimately meaningless world" (Gehlen). In two generations, we have rebuilt ourselves to profanation for all intents and purposes. No doubt about it, in hollow offensiveness we have caught up with the top of the world; when it comes to translating a lack of perspective into mobilization, we follow closely behind the major powers; in our self-doubt we have even become an exporting nation and German melancholy enjoys international prestige; all over the world, "Made in Germany" stands for a state of mind, thanks to which feelings of meaninglessness are translated into a willingness to perform. Thus we have found our connection to kinetic modernity, to the mediocre and-so-on that dreams of catastrophic interruption, to the accelerating escalators, which automatically keep moving without a need for vision and approval.

But if post-modern modernity currently suffers from doomsday nightmares, it is because it can tell that the ability to withstand the extreme is beginning to disappear. For years now, anthologies and special booklets on the apocalypse have been published all over the world. In other words, contemporaries are noting with interest that the removal of a deadline on the world process is failing. This gives us pause for thought, because it threatens the temporal-logical core of the enterprise called the modern age. The energies that once dared to carry out the infinite project of modernity on the finite base of the earth feel suddenly dramatically scarce. An awareness of being pressed for time threatens everything far more than the mid-term. The modern-day program for deadline extension once again transforms into doomsday thinking, where the impossibility to escape the logic of time makes itself deeply felt. There is even much to suggest that the sharpest edges of the last-days problematic have yet to appear before us. We are not, as it turns out, done with the fact that the wartime allies removed the hysterical millennium of Central European fascism from the world in 1945. The long postwar peace gave the victors time to settle into the irony of their victory. After the fall of the monster, it had to slowly become apparent that great powers in the modern age represent crypto-millenarian structures *per se*. This can also be seen both in the alcoholic-athletic millennium of the socialist republics of workers, peasants, and functionaries and in the melancholy baroque lifestyle millennium of North-Western European welfare states. For the hysterical Protestantism of the philanthropic World Mission of "America," this is true in a special way. Each of these entities discreetly claims a last-days status in the sense that none of them can imagine a future that would be different from their respective self-extension into infinity. Thus, as citizens of Eastern or Western great power complexes, we have reached the limits of the "classical" realm of history, and therefore cannot imagine any other morning than that of escalators, that is, the dynamic perpetuation of the conditions of movement and eternal life that the relevant mobilizers have meanwhile reached at the national or multinational level. What is the point of these reflections? It becomes apparent in the assumption that these kinds of observations reveal the temporal-logical reason for our present crisis: the conceivability of world time under the Old European historical drama patterns is approaching utter depletion. For this reason, European intelligence – where it does not evade with decisions and confessions – has been living for some time now with the awareness that it no longer has any positive terms for "what is really happening." We feel it in our nerve endings that as modernity began, so did the final act of classically conceived world time – this act is a phase that no longer wants to be a phase, but an indefinite continuum that perpetuates itself through the status quo in an irrevocable permanent self-affirmation.

Whoever has this perception of time in themselves – be it conceptualized or not – cannot be perturbed by the fact that advanced modernity simultaneously displays both claustrophobic and agoraphobic reactions. To a world that can neither date or narrate itself, every now is too cramped and too vast, while a need for space immediately merges into a fear of limitlessness. The idea that everything ends in a big bang is no more frightening than the thought that everything goes on forever.

At this point, does it make sense to ask if we can "find a way out" from the interior of the late-modern last days state of mind? Isn't it nonsense to think that we may find an "exit" into the post-historical open? Is there not an inadmissible combination of spatial images with concepts of time in such phrases? What kind of sense can speculation have of whether there is an outer realm in relation to world history up to now? Is a form of time conceivable that would be open as a dimension of depth of an essentially post-historical species life? And how should the actors of the current history finale depart from the stage of the Judeo-Christian-Western world period, when it is clear that their whole way of being and justification for existence is based on such moral-historico-dramatic concepts?

In these questions, the uncanny comes together with what is difficult to imagine. They condense three hypotheses, and each carries a dizzying historico-philosophical risk: first, that so-called "world history" in itself is the psycho-political and geopolitical result of a history-making script that was first designed in Persian-Jewish court metaphysics and then acted out by the monotheistic nations; secondly, that a more long-term future is only open to a historically highly mobilized humanity if it revises its previously valid historical script and post-historically breaks character; thirdly, that the Old European salvation-, reason-, integration-, and exoner-ation-historical conception of the world can actually be overridden and neutralized by a new, explicitly non-history-making world time schema. These theses are difficult to conceive of if their logic of time goes against the grain of a reason that represents worlds in a modern way; they are uncanny to the extent that within them everything is focused on defending the historic time bomb that ticks towards the end of the world.

The critique of historical reason – so far almost exclusively a domain of peaceful Dilthey researchers – suddenly proves to be the core of the question regarding "fate" in an age where it has been replaced by history. A critique of historical reason must therefore ultimately mean a critique of eschatological reason: that is, at the same time a critique of time-conceiving thinking, aim-thinking, anticipatory reason which imagines the end states, dramaturgical reason which stages the world process in a final act as it is written – in short, critique of the history-making reason that leads to the mobilization of the planet. All these critiques strive towards a post-historical process thinking that seeks to model the movement of the world within time minus apocalypses, final acts, consummations, arrival fantasies, final judgments, and last kingdom thoughts.

What concept of history is being used here? The world history set in motion as a drama striving to the end is linked to the fates of a super-subject that grasps all events with a continued historical effect as its own "inner context" and carries them on. For the seat of this historico-dramatic subject, only outstanding figures of salvation history or reason history are eligible: a chosen people, a world spirit, a proceeding species reason, a learning world-state central system. The content of a story belonging to such figures consists solely in the self-creation and self-realization of the subject on the world stage. Because history, understood as such, can simply be nothing more than a self-realization drama at the highest level, the whole striving, recognition, and action of the subject of history must remain curved into the interior of its self-accomplishment. Let's assume for a moment that this super-subject acted through the brains of the current mobilization carriers and said "I" and "we" through their mouths. For this subject, who of course says "for me" and "for us," the only possible reality is consequently that which belongs to its own realization. Thus, to count as "real," something must be attributable to the occurrences in which our salvation, reason, wealth, and life alleviation, to cite Bloch, are brought forth. Dramatic world time is pure self-realization time for the super-subject. For it/me/us, the world is nothing but stage and resource, fuel and building material for the progressive mobilization of the self that is realized in the movement towards further movement. Because the super-subject can in principle have nothing outside itself, it practically acts in a cosmopolitan sense. It realizes itself by tirelessly maintaining its cosmopolitan stride.

But as long as this historical drama that strives for generalization in a cosmopolitan way is in motion, the earth must stay reduced to a mere setting. Because the enterprise that is history implies from the outset the self-bending of the history-making agent nations, it is established in the script of this theatrical piece that the setting called earth must turn out to be a mere background for a historically demanding process-progress. History is *a priori* the play that makes its bill without the stage. It stems from the anti-symbiotic catastrophe that leads humans to "step out" of society. It is only through the anti-symbiotic revolution that leads to history that the human being turns into an ontological animal – something that says what is and what will become different. Because history executes its dramatic content after the exodus from symbioses of a mobilizing humanity, it is nothing other than metaphysics in action, detachment of nature through technology, staging of the epistemic-messianic process against the background of a serving and see-through earth. The drama's indifference to its setting is codified in the logic of mobilization. It is only at the moment when the play threatens to ruin the stage that the players are forced into a new self-perception. Historically moved humanity had to wait for the imperialisms of modern times, the industrial age, and planetary media civilization before seeing the truth about its own enterprise through the crisis of its fundamental position. It has had to produce the informational pantheism of news culture and the mercantile pantheism of monetized total circulation[9] in order to see that it always bumps into itself when it crosses a limit – all transcendence leads to an accelerated autism.

A post-historical era would reveal its beginning through an extroversion of the players towards their stage. After the history-making staging of one's own, the discovery of the forgotten real other is once again possible and overdue. But if we are talking about extroversion, we do not mean another willful turn towards an additional attack space, but rather care towards what has previously been taken for granted as that which merely underlies. This extroversion becomes unavoidable nowadays to the extent that what merely seems to underlie is beginning to slip away from us. Astronautics and ecology – the two ways of seeing that stand out in the current "self-thematization" of humanity – provide us with disturbing images with respect to the (fall of) earth. Since we have been able to see our planet with satellite eyes from the outside, the previously basic has become a quintessential problem case.

Our extroversion is first initiated by the catastrophe of the underlying: very obviously, the earth cannot provide for much longer what it seemed to up until now. It is overwhelmed by the role expected of it; that of *theatrum cosmopoliticum*. Its historical assignments: to serve as base camps for the historic exodus; to be available as a source of construction and fuel; to being the scene and object of geopolitical exploitation – these are no longer compatible with the earth's existence for the foreseeable future. A veritable post-story therefore begins with the growth of the earth out of its historically acquired annihilation definitions. It is hardly necessary to say that these conceptions of the earth are those of the so-called "high cultures," the height of which is consistently measured by the vastness of their repulsion from the earth-symbiotic state. It is no coincidence that cosmopolitanism is the criterion of victorious high culture; even less coincidental is the fact that the word "world-citizen," "cosmopolite," was initially a prophetic Cynical joke that was to assume a world-historical seriousness. Meanwhile, the most pronounced citizens of the world hardly still live on this earth – they have become inhabitants of the country of "complexity," members of the Grande Vitesse class, hasty through-travelers in this "Hotel Earth."

By contrast, the behavior of an earth-citizen would be one that sees the planet as more than an indifferent stage for the production of "our" play, in which we act as subjects of great promises and justifications: redemption, self-realization, time saved. It is with good reason that German parlance reserved the term "citizens of the earth" (*Erdenbürger*) for newborns, as if to mark the only moment in the life of the individual in which they are granted a hint of superiority over the historical world. Perhaps it is not entirely meaningless that it was an astronaut, Edgar Mitchell ("the sixth man on the moon"), who gave the term new content when he described the sentiments of those returned from outer space: "Each man comes back with a feeling he is no longer only an American citizen; he is a planetary citizen." Should there really be an era "after history," its opening would be inseparable from the advent of the earth out of its historical way of being as curtain and raw material and with its illumination as the content of human devotion and care. The earth as a global object, previously lifted and hidden in the darkness of our closeness to it, has since been brought before itself through a series of technically historical "levers" and "spins"; it now sees itself with artificial and natural eyes on. This changes all the premises of the historical game. What was once the scene becomes the theme of the plot. What served as a background comes to the forefront. What was present as a raw material emerges as product. What was previously stage becomes the play itself. Such are the axioms of a post-historical dramaturgy in which the rules of the game are formulated according to a corresponding post-politics. Whatever may be played "on" the old earth stage, it itself is increasingly providing the subject matter of the plays. But it can already be said that "world history" as a time project for the acting out of spiritual and moral missions in front of natural and physical backgrounds is an exhausted idea. If philosophy of history is still to be good for something, then surely it is to comment on the meaning of the exhaustion of the history-making idea. This critical theory of history sabotages world-historical dramaturgy, just as history previously stepped into the world as an initiative for the sabotaging of fate. After the force of fate, a world-historical compulsion is now to be subverted – the play does not have to be played to the end. This insight comes too soon from the perspective of a history that wants to culminate; only through its seduction, however, is it able to postpone the annihilating culmination. By coming too soon, it stands with respect to temporal logic in the right place to disrupt the automatisms at whose entrance it would be too late. That is why it remains superfluous to wait for the dawn of apocalyptic anger, nor will anyone experience the Victory Day of a last kingdom. What emerges before us in the logic of procedural time can only be an era without the metaphysical difference between timeless earth stage and historical human drama. For us, the old "nature" no longer exists as a massive pedestal of cosmic pre-performance that would be preset for all human time. For us, the earth is no longer the endlessly patient "building and carrying" that it appeared to be to almost all previous generations. It is precisely through the historical process and its two main events, large-scale technology and the human rights mission, that the earth has been destabilized in its carrying. What once meant nature and was placed in opposition to cultural institutions as a pre-human totality has since been included within the maelstrom of human constructions. If what was once called "nature" had managed to stay alive, its existence would no longer be due to its self-sufficiency – it lost that a few centuries ago via its apprehension by a technically powerful scientific spirit. It can only survive thanks to a new world-building gesture, carried out by people for whom it has become evident that looking after the stage is the play itself.

To what extent do the outlines of a post-historical principle of reality surface in these considerations? By principle of reality we mean the obligations of thought and behavior that develop in human cultures under the afflux of chronic stress and danger. By bowing to the *principium realitatis*, consciousness adjusted to the burdensome and risky nature of existence. Because there are fundamentally different attitudes to difficulty and risk, there are more than superficial differences between human cultures. It is even more clear than in their deeply different languages that different cultures manifest their mode of being in the world through the very different ways they bear its weight. Each culture develops its special gesture to master the heavy and precarious, its own style of dealing with the inevitable, its own cunning in the repeal of the unbreakable, its own rules of play for making the unbearable bearable. That is why it is true for all cultures what Herbert Marcuse tries to demonstrate for the modern world: the principle of reality is not only and not for all times identical to the indomitable law of need that restricts and burdens lives in cruel indifference. The approaches to what we now call history in the singular lie in the universally instigated struggles of civilizations against the burdening character of world conditions, and if the compass of all truly history-making traveling beings points to the pole of freedom, it is because freedom is inextricably

associated with relief in the imaginations of "developed" civilizations. Europe became "the mother of revolutions" because it is the
original theatrical continent, the primary scene of an ontological
revolt against the weight of the world, the stage of an inner-worldly
liberation project that advertises with the promise to break the
foreign rule of a dejected need of life through self-determined work.

In the principle of reality of the Christian age, the hopes of the
individual were primarily directed to their personal redemption
and with a psycho-politics of patience, converted into a willingness
to endure the given. But a salvational-dramatic time arc was also
extended, which virtually forced all of humanity into a political-
theological community of destiny. In this way, an imperial, expansive
history-making motif was formed into the Christian modeling of the
principle of reality. From the sixteenth century, the explosive power of
this is reflected in the Catholically legitimized imperialisms through
which the planetary stride of Christianity begins. At the same time,
ascetic Protestantism began a new salvation-economic offensive in
which economic success impulses were linked to religious election
motifs. Both arrangements, Catholicizing geopolitics and Protestant
Profit Yoga, pair earthly traffic forces with sacred commands. From
then on, the path is open for modern kinetic pantheism, which uses
capitals, texts, vehicles, and radio waves to strive for the total lique-
faction of all that is solid and standing.

It is only in the success story of this kinetic pantheism that the
ominous "project of modernity" becomes possible. If modernity is
indeed a project, and not just drift and growth, it has a great ambition
to claim reality as its own design. Where essential modernity reigns,
reality only rhymes with self-realization. That is why reality in
the old-ontological sense is an unacceptable, reactionary word to
modern ears. Those who live inside the Western modernization
cyclone, spoiled by success, are already taking part in a revolution of
relief that has long since overtaken all traditional standards for what
is unavoidable and to be withstood. The classical components of the
old principle of reality: unbendingness of the law, unpredictability
of fate, intransigence of suffering – within modernity, all are, if not
rendered ineffective, then certainly reduced to a residual size. The
ontological revolt of modernity sets a threefold upheaval in motion
against these "constants": a mobilization revolution; a safeguarding
revolution; a revolution of motion generation and unburdening.
Revolutionary modernity can dream of the establishment of a
"world" in which all independent resistance to the sovereign outlet
of the mobilized self would have been lifted because it rejects reality
– the unstoppable resistance *per se* – as a reactionary principle.
In the kinetic pantheism of such an accomplished modernity, as

the young Schelling suspected, infinite self-activity would coincide with absolute calmness, neo-worldly prometheanism would descend into epicurean detachment, principled activism would have to melt into an ultimate quietism. Only under the pull of such pantheistically paradisiacal alluring images could the modern philosophy of progress break the old principle of reality and replace the ages-old politics of guilt with an unprecedented impatient politics of disinhibition and unburdening. These, too, are reasons to characterize modernity as a stealthy eschaton: its principle of reality can be about nothing more than the last effort at a happiness-political removal of what still requires effort.

What the Christian-medieval version of the principle of reality has in common with modern times is that both perceive nature as an ahistorical background of human drama – even if modernity no longer sees it as a history of salvation, but a program for self-preservation, progress, and self-enhancement. Even where these specifically history-making versions of the reality principle are in force, human actors remain introverted in their worries of redemption and relief. Their drama takes place against a natural backdrop and on a planetary stage, drawing from a natural fund and disassembling uncovered physical riches for the benefit of human assembling. Pushed by archaic fear and inspired by modern design power, the subjects of the modern project draw basic raw materials and energy sources into their pragmatic dramas as props, that is, as mobile accessories. Their "work" transforms "matter" into consumables for their great scenarios, which revolve around world domination, humanization, growth, self-realization, redemption, and relief. Wherever history is made in this sense, there can be no question of an appreciation of the earth as a "reality" in its own right. It is always used like a self-evident, non-dramatic basis for unlikely, dramatic superstructures and expeditions. But this attitude of laying claim is now on the verge of disaster. What currently creates epochs is the revenge of the former background on the depicted figures and frameworks: the background has emerged from its inconspicuousness and quit its assigned position as supplier of self-evident things. The old ecology of stage and play is out of joint. It is now no longer possible to place ruthlessly risky cultural figures on endlessly resilient natural slides. The slide itself demands that its previously overlooked improbability enter into the figures it carries and be considered in them. It might even seem that nature took revenge on history by having its own fragility suddenly surpass the riskiness of the historical structure. Thus, the due de-dramatization of history gives prelude to the rediscovery of a dramatic nature. If humanity were to awaken from its historical narcissism, it would discover that it no longer has a mission other than to make the concern of an overly finite nature its own. By way of historical mobilization successes, nature and civilization have grown together into a common improbability. To perceive reality under such conditions is to profess solidarity in the improbable. Where this perception is clarified, an earth-bourgeois ethos spontaneously arises. The maxim of human action must now always be able to lead to the avoidance of further blind impositions on the carrying capacity of the earth. The old base, contrary to its name, cannot easily be claimed as a basis that bears any structure. Meanwhile, it depends for its part on the "adherence" of constructions to the fundamental nature of their basic situation and on being let to be more than a self-evident underlying of things. Just as everything that is built up has always been in need of a basis, so too has the basis become construction-dependent. Since then, an abyssal caveat has been mixed into the horizontal position of the basic: even what is lying down can still fall. Cultural theory crosses an epochal threshold as soon as it understands the new fact from which to begin, namely that base and construction irrevocably form a community of fragility from now on. From that moment on, the world-historical drama is translated back into prehistoric perspectives. Global history is transformed from the singular cosmopolitan self-realization project into a pluralistic earth-bourgeois household problem. This obtains via force a philosophical economy of ecology. The fact that the earth explodes today as the "whole house" of life is itself the result of the singular, globalizing, dramatic history. The historical large-scale attempt to establish the "house of man" on a universal scale has caused both deserts and islands of prosperity to grow. Again, this is just another way of saying that it turned out differently with the historical enterprise than we thought. Can history itself be thought of as the event in which things have to turn out differently? Is it predestined for failure as long as it makes its calculation without movement? Doesn't the phenomenon of history result *a priori* from the conflict between project and drift, step and fall? If it behaves in this way, then the sharpness of this contradiction would also be a measure of the distance between the initial intentions and the final results within the historical process. That could not be any bigger today. Because the distance between what was wanted and what occurred lays painfully open in the consciousness of contemporaries, the supposition arises in their minds that it could all go terribly wrong with the entire historical world. We no longer feel comfortable in our historical skin since history increasingly turns out to be the means by which it all goes wrong "in the end."

But since when did the risk of it all going wrong (turning out "false") come into play – where did the danger of falsification come from? With such questions, current thinking repeats a concern for the truth and untruth of the whole, through the appearance of which the highly cultural level of human thought is announced. In the sheer question of how what came to be could come to be, that is, in the pre-Socratic explosion of the question of "emergence as such," the truth problem arises as vehemently as possible before the world-imagining consciousness. The question of truth becomes the no longer provable problem in the history-founding moment where the impression comes to the forefront of the threat that it could all go wrong with the way of the world. Does an original correspondence between the consciousness of human history and the risk of falsehood (i.e. wrongness) in the course of the world therefore exist? Perhaps the opposite is more correct: that the aberrations of the world course are linked from the very beginning to the emergence of imaginatively gifted beings whose answer to the depressing evidence of their false life is a series of history-making drafts of a true world that is to be sought. Unmistakably, all paths to the false, fake, and wrong converge in the human – that *homo sapiens sapiens* who at the beginning of their high-cultural era is gripped by the compulsion to ask after the truth. For this being, the partiality of the question becomes inescapable because they learn from their own upsets that they are the being who does not fit. The question of truth dawns on them because they discover themselves in the focal point of the palpably wrong. It is only in their ability to get it completely wrong that humans become aware of an ontological privilege that the philosophers have wrapped into that darkly dazzling word "freedom." Freedom is not only serenity towards the real, in which – as Heidegger wisely indicated – the "essence of truth" lies, but also the disembarkation into the risk-filled, which includes multiple experiences of the false and fake since the ominous "going astray" manifests itself in a variety of ways: from the abyss of the fearsome strangeness between soul and world to the "regional" variants of falseness which we know as dissonance, misfit, faltering, dissent, unfoundedness, and forfeit. Early on, the first philosophies moved humans themselves towards the source of the First Wrong, or directly identified them with it: be it that they attached themselves to the wrong principle in the primal dispute between light and dark, helped the actually unjustified to a deceptive existence via an existing error, or broke out of an initial state of unity by way of collapse, hubris, rebellion, or forgetting. It is only once spirit has been impregnated by falseness that it recognizes itself in the conspicuous urge to set up its existence on safe founda-tions. As it builds its structures, it thus wants to use the substance from which indestructible certainty is made. That substance is truth, because it promises to be what preserves itself in a collapse, what stays as opposed to flees, what is fundamental in contrast to what is imposed. Truth is the axe with which the continuum of beings will be split into the primary and the secondary – absolute principles and secondary cases, sure origins and endangered derivatives, eternal axioms and fleeting connections. By way of metaphysical shamanism, human acts and institutions ought to be "set up" on primordial models and first foundations, so that a transfer of being, power, and safety can arise from the ground up. The more fragile the foundation, the more strenuous the base-laying magic spell.

The metaphysical ways of thinking, as handed down from their beginnings in the axes of time, testify to a shocking increase in consciousness from the disintegration tendency of man-made orders. The oldest documents of these logics that search within an absolute halt necessarily stem from the early days of states and countries. Where power grows to gasping heights for the first time, people, as rulers as well as victims, begin to gain experiences with a new quality of risk. That is why the state, metaphysics, and fear of falling are formations of the same age. At the time when these phenomena take shape, the mythical memories of Golden Ages and Paradise Expulsions also find the form in which they have been handed down to this day. Such narratives testify to the moment when a consciousness captured by the pull of history looks back and gets overwhelmed by the evidence that whatever makes history is worse than what does not. To plunge forward into time is to progress downward into the wrong: this is a primordial self-interpretation of the life that has become historic. The myth of the Golden Age presupposes the historically powerful distinction between a high time and a declining one. It contrasts prehistoric homeostasis with historical descent. While "in the beginning" the measure of things consisted of voluntary nature, gentleness, and durability, as a result of the myth, the old "world order" corrodes itself in a progressive decay down to iron conditions. Here, coercion, brutalization, and uncertainty are so characteristic that, as soon as it is mentioned, we know immediately: this concerns us. What's more, history-affirming pragmatic thinking seeks to dismiss these myths as a first romance. The correct skeptical remark that, in reality, there never "was" a Golden Age of humanity is meaningless alongside the fact that some cultures that drift into history have truly found their way through the ages of the world to be one of decline. This inner view of the historical existence was occasionally able to get a few words in edgewise, where the need to praise what happened was not totally effective. This marked the scene of an initial cultural criticism. These cannot be separated from the realistic, if futile, lament about the risks and deformations of a life oriented towards politics. Even Daniel's vision of the colossus on clay feet – a historical prophetic image of the effect of a self-making history – shows how, in the erection period of the high culture consciousness, the insight into the connection between increased power and increasing fragility emerged at the same time. Almost two and a half millennia after Daniel, this connection is more visible than ever, with the difference that, in addition to the classical arthritis of the great powers, new aspects of fragility have emerged that seem so pregnant with disaster that they make the downfall of the Mesopotamian Empire appear somatically soothing. "World history" as a process/progress that sets up risky cultural figures on the stable foundations of nature and truth has meanwhile come close to a point where it has to swear an oath of disclosure as a wrong history.

As the basic gesture of metaphysical as well as technical constructing, erecting to stand upright is at the same time the history-making wrongness which draws the foundation into the fate of untenable structures. This is why the world history of human falsehood is both more than and different from an exception of biological law, according to which the mis-adaptation of species is evolutionarily countered with their extinction. When it comes to humans – the constructive, ontological animal – a fulfilled wrong history would not only lead to a collapse of the set-up and the extinction of the species, it would also drag the foundations into the demise of the superstructures and allow what underlies the set-up to be part of its collapse. If the erection of structures wants to be more than just a daring straightening up of one's posture, but rather strives towards a "safeguarding of establishments," it turns into a gesture of the first error; it ends up there because it compulsively performs a gesture of denial against an already experienced fall. In the form of this gesture, it is at the heart of what subjectivity means. The basic statement is the criminal lie of the active subject, which, at the height of its unfolding, covers the whole earth with untenable structures. With respect to the erected structure, it is not the vertical pull that is false – a pull that cannot be removed from the thought of a right human mobility. The forgery arises from the securely standing pose, which wants to give the uninsured life a stand of its own on unwavering foundations. "If it had been possible to build the Tower of Babel without climbing it, it would have been permitted."[10]

The earth, as a locality for the symbioses of common improbabilities, is not a principle, not a fundament. The way the earth sustains living forms has nothing to do with the relationship between base and building. Its sustaining of them is a making possible, not a securing. This sustaining enfolds alongside the gestures of birth – bearing, bringing forth, raising up, setting free. There is no basis for any type of grounding in the play of these gestures – supporting and daring are one and the same in them; in coming to be, passing away comes to be known at the same time. It is only through the gestures of a production of safeguards that stir up in the metaphysical animal that the historically powerful opposition between ecology and ontology arises. It is only through the securing gestures of production that rouse from within the metaphysical animal that the history-making contrast between the ecological and the ontological breaks up. Ecology adheres to the naturalness of nature[11] by recognizing the state of being sustained and supported in all occurring life forms. On the other hand, ontology is entangled in the architectural adventure of high cultures: it executes the compulsion for ever more universal production, which Heidegger defined as the fate of the "*Gestell*" – a placing to stand upright and an enframing.[12] If a fateful greatness is recognized in the empowerment to construction, it is because with the emancipation of constructing, the compulsion to make history and suffer has also come into force at the same time. That is why history remains until the end only the continuation of the fall from symbiosis by other means. It does on a large scale what the individual life tries do on a smaller one – transform separation into autonomy, fall into construction, disaster into project. It is always the anti-symbiotic powers that make history in the true sense of the word. History is the effort to rework the disadvantage of being born into an advantage of self-realization. Only when the discontent with self-generation begins to border on the unbearable will humans also regain the advantage of being born.

For an Ontology of Still-Being

> In Paradise, I would not last a "season" or even a day; then how account for my nostalgia for it? I don't account for it, it has inhabited me always, it was part of me before I was.
> E.M. Cioran, *The Trouble with Being Born*[13]

Ever since the first historical human being lifted their head, times have been stubbornly interesting. Not a day goes by without a disaster, not a year without novelty, no generation without departures towards hope against one's better judgment. High culture may speak of itself because it moves very much in the element of "event." As long as it sets up worlds that want to continue being narrated, it insists on being made from the stuff of heroic epics and novel series.

The degree to which high culture is interesting corresponds precisely to the degree of civilizational mobilization – the interesting is the psychological interest rate of the catastrophe. Once the interesting drug called history has grasped the entire psyche, it appears as something we can no longer imagine being without. Overwhelmed by its own movement, the thinking avalanche sets itself in motion, following a self-potentializing dynamic that is peculiar to the subjects of the world process who are on their way to more power and skill. Where the very historicity of existence becomes unfastened, it takes on the structure of a history-making history – it continually acquires its agents, through which it continually keeps going and casts itself forward in an increasingly heightened way. That is why the essential historical consciousness is not so much defined by traditionalism (which essentially remains ahistorical) but the tradition of mobilization. History organizes itself like a rally in time, which searches for its route from stage to stage even if it often gets the impression that there is no more path to continue on. The history-making teams have fallen as willfully as the suicidal mob of the Paris–Dakar rally. Frenetically, they are on their way from Babylon to Megalopolis, and time and again they find their manic whisperers indulging them in the idea of being race leaders and sponsors in the formidable enterprise – prophets, philosophers of history, moralists, theorists of learning, great men of the highest mission. Just as the interesting is the psychological interest rate of the catastrophe, so too are the missions its loans. Where history has begun as a self-fulfilling mission, the not-yet-structure begins to reign, mobilizing life with unfulfilled orders. The mission-dynamic constitution of essential history condemns any historically achieved state of affairs to embarrass itself before what has not yet been achieved. Everything that is now is latently destroyed by being measured against what is still to come: because the appearance of the not-yet-being always prevails for the utopian-missionary gaze of current beings, the real is degraded to the mere appearance of a being that first has arrived in order to exist. The already-arrived is obliterated by the not-yet-fulfilled. In the process, the insatiable hunger for the future grows.

The ontology of the not-yet-being – magnificently defined by Ernst Bloch – gives away the secret of the historical mobilization of the world. It outlines an ontology of the becoming being, which determines the world process as a genre drama that lifts itself upwards to the highest leitmotifs. This processes from within itself the agents, engines, and motivations as a by-product, through which it can then launch itself into even further spaces of not-yet-being. As the ontology of the revolutionary world movement, Bloch's teaching, which has not yet become a utopian goal, rationalizes world history as a space of increase in an infinite mission: where the world was, God should become. But because the real world must never be directly divine, but at most provide the initial letter of the divine name, the becoming-God of the world is at the same time given to infinite postponement. Thus, the currently real ontologically finds itself in a quandary: as a "comprising of," it is obsolete and devalued from the outset; as a mobilization-making mass, it is placed at the disposal of benefiting accelerated improvements, which time and again lead to the incorrigible.

In the ontology of not-yet-being, the restlessness of historical injured life is theorized as a history-making hope. With the help of a mission-ontological boost, the drivenness transforms itself into promise and charges back into itself as a will to non-release. It is this self-drive that turns suffering from reality into an engine for the departure into the New World of modern times. If the ontological definition of modern times as a being-towards-movement has become universal for us in this matter, it is due to the fact that modern times are synonymous with the phenomenon that it is only a few centuries ago that enterprising humans were able to achieve an effective interconnection of mission motifs and technical success machines. This success, which triggered avalanches of further success, meanwhile spins over into its own successes. Since the beginning of modern times, historical acceleration phenomena have experienced a nuclear-like increase. This means nothing more than that the self-intensification loops responsible for modern mobilizations have become conclusive on a broad front in recent centuries. Only when imagination principally imagines itself (as in the transcendental philosophies), the will wills itself (as in the pragmatic power ontologies), productivity is produced (as in the liberal or socialistically motivated industrial systems), and creativity is created (as in psycho-technical stimulation of "ingenious" obsessions) – only then will history makers be systematically launched and mobilizers published in series. These dangerously multiplied perpetrators are increasingly responsive to each other and to their offensive projects and campaigns. The "events" generated by them condense into a catastrophic jelly. The apparent learning process is turning into a real nuclear process. The further this escalates, the more desperate the Old Enlightenment affirmations sound which claim that humanity today still moves within a prehistory of itself. History's conception as an infinite mission now forces its agents into great bold positions: while most signs in the world point to a not-long-now, they must stubbornly hold onto the still-not-yet. But maybe they're right. Between the previous not-yet and the imminent no-more, we poor interim devils are only left with the unhappy awareness that we have always lived in the wrong time. We are too late for the first paradise and too early for the second. A history that can until the last only be a pre-history of fulfilled times is for us nothing other than a lost time.

What was claimed at the beginning of the book on modernity – that it represents the paradoxical program to carry out an infinite project on a finite basis – can now be said about history as a whole, insofar as it proceeds in an anthropogonic exodus, as a utopian way home and an apocalyptic mobilization. The history-making tension between the design and the foundation, between the driving and the persisting, is not only based on the non-relationship between the infinite and finite, the utopian and the topical. Far more powerfully effective in it is the act of confusing the memory of an intra-uterine, a-cosmically blessed existence with the anticipation of an extra-uterine, worldly-real universal happiness. In the historical ontological phantasm of the self-illuminating not-yet, an a-cosmic past is projected onto a cosmic future, the intra-uterine dowry is hallucinated as an outer defiant world. But then history can be nothing other than the endless birth struggle of a phantasmagorical human body that is abandoned by the inner-motherly homeland and exposed to non-motherly foreignness. There it has to throw itself into the enterprise of turning the foreign into a home. But the foreign never quite wants to be the same as that which is our own and our home. Because the a-cosmic cannot be "realized" in the cosmic – because world-less limbo is never the result of worldwide effort – the historic departure towards the realization of the real home must be an extermination campaign against the immediately present, cosmic, outer, others. The matricide undertaken to extort a return to the womb is the logical and objective consequence of this "world-historical" directive of the *experimentum mundi*.

Once the a-cosmic character of the utopian ideal becomes clear, we can see through the temporal-logical deception upon which the ontology of the not-yet-being rests. The miraculous pull of the very other – that storm from paradise that drives into the wings of Walter Benjamin's angel of history[14] – comes from a "place" that does not lie before us but behind us. That is why today's search for the future is a catastrophic misunderstanding – the paradise-political raid of nature as raw material which does not know how things happen to it – paradise now. "This cannot be achieved with the nature that is given, but also not, as empty dreams of soul would claim, without nature. The dream of a better life means at long last, *in toto*, a new world, that is, again a setting, a cosmic country."[15] As soon as the deception is lifted, the temporal sense of the utopian changes: it is not approaching towards us from the future; rather,

it is the light of the "still" that is cast from an undeniably given life
also into the ungiven. That is why the "still" is more powerful than
the not-yet. The spirit of utopia belongs less to the self-illuminating
becoming of something better than to the still itself luminiferous
still-being of what has been begun. Nothing is revealed within it,
but it has an afterglow. From this correction onward, no one can
get near the utopian "small town" if they approach it as if it were
something that has yet to be opened: the utopian "place" can only
be "arrived at" by a "turn" back into the still open. Those who
come into the still open are not pursuing something distant, but
allow themselves to be caught up with by the unreachably near. In
the still-being, the true spirit of utopia blows, which must not want
its own "realization" without misunderstanding itself. Freed from
the illusions of attainment, the incomparable unplace proves to be a
resting point. Because utopia can no longer be thought of as a goal
or mission statement, the previously mobilizing itself now becomes
the seat of demobilization. Only those who know what it means
to have nothing left to do have a criterion for the right mobility.
Instead of mass mobilizations forward, fully movable floating in
the here and now becomes possible. The way of critique passes
over into a critique of the way. The not yet achieved gets to know
the truly achievable in the still-being. Thus, the idea of critique
must be based on a newly understood spirit of utopia. In doing so,
critique as ability to make a difference discovers its premise in the
possibility of having nothing to critique. The difference between
difference and non-difference sets the "more thoughtful thinking"
in motion, which can stay moving even if the totality-theoretical
phantasm of an identification of identity and non-identity should
prove unfeasible. As critiquing subjects, we are not only the bearers
of the ability to make distinctions, but rather much more still
those who are themselves differentiated and who think from a
place of separation – only because we, as differentiated ones, as
individualized spirits, can presuppose the fetal non-differentiation
are we as born subjects differentiation-competent. However, the
first difference, which makes a distinction as such, is due not to
the use of discernment, but to the miraculous catastrophe of
the coming-into-the-world. While monistic metaphysicians absorb
the Absolute into a fetal imagination in order to absorb the
worldly other into the world-less One, dramatic critique follows the
coming-into-the-world of that which thinks; on the screen of fetal
remembrance, it carries on the adventure of being different. That
is why a real critical theory, should it exist one day, will be identical
to authentic mysticism. As a living difference between worldlessness
and worldliness, the unique existence will become aware of its

being-in-the-world. The spirit of cosmopolitanism will come to see itself as an enlightened a-cosmism. Only the mystical path will then still be open. As a critique of the path, it leads to where we are.

Notes

Premises

1 [The original German title of this book is *Eurotaoismus: Zur Kritik der politischen Kinetik* (Frankfurt: Suhrkamp, 1989).]
2 In the following, especially pp. 66ff.
3 Cf. Peter Sloterdijk, *Zur Welt kommen – Zur Sprache kommen* (Frankfurt: Suhrkamp, 1988).
4 [Franz Kafka, *A Hunger Artist and Other Stories*, trans. Joyce Crick (Oxford: Oxford University Press, 2012), p. 192.]

Chapter 1 The Modern Age as Mobilization

1 [The original German edition was published in 1989.]
2 Unless we accept the identification of the world with the adversary *par excellence* – as Ernst Bloch did in his old age when he at last put his gnostic cards on the table: see *Experimentum Mundi: Frage, Kategorien des Herausbringens, Praxis* (Frankfurt: Suhrkamp, 1975), Chapter 45, "Aufklärung und Teufelsglaube, die Fortdauer des Widersacherischen."
3 It was Marx who first saw through the moral mystification of the kinetic. He found not so much that Kant's "moral law" falls into the interiority of a sense of duty, but that it is conscience that allows itself to be mobilized as a duty to revolution. The categorical imperative is therefore less an ethical sentence than a kinetic sentence: it says less about what you *should* do than what you have to *overthrow* in order to be able to do it, namely all circumstances that inhibit human kinetic.
4 [Jean-Paul Sartre, *Existentialism is a Humanism*, trans. Carol Macomber (New Haven: Yale University Press, 2007), p. 29.]
5 Traditionally, spirit has a precarious relationship with movement – except that we say of it that it blows where it wants to (which is probably to be understood as a compliment to the inspired and also

meant to explain that there is nothing we can do in the event of a lull). If we want to understand this relationship in positive terms, it could be provisionally characterized by five criteria: contextuality (spirit is aware of the goings-on outside itself), self-perception (it intuits itself), self-limitation (it realizes when it is enough), reversibility (it has "play," it can do what it can, back and forth), and spontaneity (it is capable not only of carrying on as before, but also of starting afresh, even surprising itself if necessary). These criteria only jointly guarantee the effect of the spiritual – separated from each other, they guarantee only intelligent stupidities (e.g. our life as it is).

6 [Novalis, *Philosophical Writings*, trans. Margaret Mahony Stoljar (Albany: State University of New York Press, 1997), p. 144.]

7 The posthumously published small work by Jacob Taubes, *Ad Carl Schmitt – Gegenstrebige Fügung* (Berlin: Merve, 1987), is an example of a free handling of another evil man of the twentieth century, namely Carl Schmitt, the thinker of world war.

8 One may note that these sentences are not formulated in the spirit of utopia, but in the spirit of system function theory, which is known to serve "conservative" interests, but here only the bare minimum of preservation, self-preservation as a non-suicide.

9 In Jacques Derrida's original formulation – *il n'ya pas de hors-texte* – the same sounds somewhat more appetizing; one hears the suspending (in our terms: de-mobilizing) function of the thesis. See Jacques Derrida, *Of Grammatology*, trans. Gayatri Chakravorty Spivak (Baltimore: Johns Hopkins University Press, 1976).

10 [Karl Marx and Friedrich Engels, *The Communist Manifesto* (Oxford: Oxford University Press, 1992), p. 6.]

11 In this context, we must draw attention to the little-known work by Dieter Claessens, *Das Konkrete und das Abstrakte: Soziologische Skizzen zur Anthropologie* (Frankfurt: Suhrkamp, 1980), which raises the question of the encroaching of an evolutionary wisdom in the sense of a "withdrawal of untenable positions" without concession to the romantic demonization of technology.

12 [Paul Valéry, "The European," in *History and Politics*, trans. Denise Folliot and Jackson Matthews, *The Collected Works, Vol. 10* (New York: Bollingen Foundation, 1962), p. 323.]

13 [Horace, *Satires and Epistles*, trans. John Davie (Oxford: Oxford University Press, 2011), p. 99.]

14 The French Indian connoisseur Raymond Schwab was, among other things, the first to draw a parallel between the adventures of Indology and the philological sensations of Renaissance Hellenism. Cf. *The Oriental Renaissance: Europe's Rediscovery of India and the East, 1680–1880*, trans. Gene Patterson-King and Victor Reinking (New York: Columbia University Press, 1984).

15 Otto Petras, *Post Christum: Streifzüge durch die geistige Wirklichkeit* (Berlin: Widerstands-Verlag, 1935), p. 11. In our final essay (pp. 129ff.), compare the remarks about Paul as the initiator of the Holy Mobilization on Christian world history. Both references, which refer to Petras as well as to Paul, are based on suggestions with which Jacob Taubes conveyed to the author a concept of the span of Jewish

historical theology. See Jacob Taubes, *Occidental Eschatology*, trans. David Ratmoko (Stanford: Stanford University Press, 2009).

16 [Novalis, *Philosophical Writings*, p. 111.]

Chapter 2 The Other Change: On the Philosophical Situation of Alternative Movements

1 [Robert Musil, *The Enthusiasts*, trans. Andrea Simon (New York: Performing Arts Journal Publications, 1983), p. 34.]

2 There is only one significant attempt to take the term "panic" philosophically seriously, the one that Hermann Broch made in his *Massenwahntheorie: Beiträge zur einer Psychologie der Politik* (Frankfurt: Suhrkamp, 1979). This attempt was born from the impression of fascism. Broch diagnoses that the real fears that affected large parts of the Central European population, especially the German population, after the First World War triggered pre-panicked conditions. In these, full-panicked energies already announce their eruption. Full panic means negative ecstasy; in it, a metaphysical despair is experienced: constriction of the self in world loss, doomsday plight, deadly isolation. Human activity is capable of the worst under the influence of "panicked" conditions – especially when the panicked energy channels itself forward into delusional programs of a breakthrough. The only counterpower that can absorb these energies, according to Broch, is the rational ecstasy in which the individual is restrained to the insight: I am the world. For Broch, it is a criterion of authentic religion that it overcomes the existential primal in rational ecstasies, while it is typical of demonic revival movements that they seduce one with destructive intoxications. Only from rational ecstasies can people make life covenants in the face of death: at first a religious, then immediately also a politically moral social contract with all contemporaries.

These speculations can be continued today in a birth-psychoanalytic way. A political perinatalism is necessary. The moment of coming into the world is at the same time a moment of fear of death for human children; it contains a lifelong, effective reservoir of panic. As social crisis pressures rise, humanity's fear of annihilation can discharge into collective negative ecstasies: suicide programs from a panicked fear of death. In a culture of coming into the world that balances political, therapeutic, and religious motives in the right ratio, the panic of world loss would be transformed into the ecstasy of coming into the world. Where this work is consciously undertaken, there can be talk of panicked culture – it must be called as such, because one has to start with the initial explosive affect situation and not with uplifting goals.

3 In just a few years, this way of thinking has been officially adopted. At the Aspen Institute's Berlin seminar on "prospects for the twenty-first century," President Richard von Weizsäcker said, referring to the New York stock market crash in October 1987, that it was "one of those small disasters that we so desperately need in order to understand how we can avert major disasters." Quoted in *Die Presse*, October 29, 1987, p. 2.

4 [A rewriting of the phrase by Karl Kraus: "Let chaos be welcome; for order has failed." Karl Kraus, *Die Fackel*, no. 285–6, 1909, p. 16.]

5 A monument of this erroneousness is Martin Heidegger's 1930 essay *The Essence of Truth*, trans. Ted Sadler (New York: Continuum, 2002). In it, the crisis of reason-that-makes-right punctures the classical district of truth, insofar as the latter had been understood as correctness, adequation, and (im)partibility. Behind it, a realm of events of (un)truth opens up, which occur as being-historical unconcealment instances with a sovereign lack of criteria.

6 All these negations are historically valid: previously not so. It remains to be seen whether the perception of these deficiencies can create an equivalent for that which was previously missing.

7 [Hugo von Hofmannsthal, "Manche freilich ...," trans. Scott Horton, *Harper's Magazine* (November 10, 2007). The following verse extracts are also from this source.]

8 [Massimo Cacciari, *The Necessary Angel*, trans. Miguel E. Vatter (Albany: State University of New York Press, 1994), p. 53.]

9 The fusion of the cannibal titan Kronos with Chronos, the running time, had already occurred in ancient times.

10 [E.M. Cioran, *The New Gods*, trans. Richard Howard (Chicago: University of Chicago Press, 2002), pp. 35–6.]

11 This lack of differentiation from what is being critiqued is something that the neo-Marxist critique has thoroughly in common with classical mobilization Marxism.

12 On this, Charles Baudelaire is the crown witness of aesthetic modernism: "At every minute we are crushed by the idea and the sensation of time. And there are only two means of escaping this nightmare, – to forget it: Pleasure and Work. Pleasure consumes us. Work fortifies us. Let us choose. [...] One can forget time only by using it." *My Heart Laid Bare and Other Texts*, trans. Rainer J. Hanshe (New York: Contra Mundum Press, 2017), p. 55.

13 This expression, which seemingly names something self-evident, does not belong to the vocabulary of philosophy – a treacherous fact. As a neologism, it is an art word from the second half of this century. We find it first with Hans Saner in the book *Geburt und Phantasie: Von der natürlichen Dissidenz des Kindes* (Basel: Lenos, 1979). However, it is prepared by Hannah Arendt's meditations on human "natality" in her main work *The Human Condition* (Chicago: University of Chicago Press, 1958).

14 The emphasis here is that both must succeed in order to maintain nature–poiesis continuity. Because the two gestures are separated from each other in the prevailing gender-ontological system, the sexual designs of man and woman are each equipped with mutilated ontological features: "man" comes into the world but brings nothing into the world; "woman" brings something into the world but does not come into the world. This scandal runs deeper than the gender segregation that the Platonic androgyny myth speaks of; the scandalous thing about it is thus also not solved by eroticism or sexual union, but only by a poietic addition: through women learning to come into the world and men learning to bring into the world.

Chapter 3 Eurotaoism?

1 [Friedrich Nietzsche, *On the Genealogy of Morality*, trans. Carol Diethe (Cambridge: Cambridge University Press, 2006), p. 25.]

2 From this point of view, there is a common denominator for Marx's theory of revolution and Nietzsche's doctrine of creative forgetting. Both doctrines want to disperse the decay of life at the hands of the past with the means of active nihilism and both rely on self-intensification in order to do so: Marx through a project that once again gives living work priority over the dead, Nietzsche by unleashing a "leonine" will to oneself with the prospect of a child-like second innocence.

3 [Michael Ende, *The Neverending Story*, trans. Ralph Manheim (Harmondsworth: Penguin Books, 1983), p. 48.]

4 [Ende, *Neverending Story*, p. 48.]

5 [Ende, *Neverending Story*, pp. 48–9.]

6 [Motto from "Selections from the Papers to the Devil" to Jean Paul Friedrich Richter, *The Invisible Lodge*, trans. Charles T. Brooks (New York: Henry Holt, 1883).]

7 [See note 3.]

8 [Nietzsche, *Genealogy of Morality*, pp. 35–7.]

9 [Karl Marx, *Early Political Writings*, ed. and trans. Joseph O'Malley and Richard A. Davis (Cambridge: Cambridge University Press, 1994), p. 82.]

10 [Nietzsche, *Genealogy of Morality*, p. 25.]

11 [Karl Marx, "Economic and Philosophic Manuscripts," in *Karl Marx: Selected Writings*, ed. David McLellan (Oxford: Oxford University Press, 1977), p. 95.]

12 [Nietzsche, *Genealogy of Morality*, p. 24.]

13 [Nietzsche, *Genealogy of Morality*, p. 80.]

14 Nietzsche's tragedy is probably to be understood from the paradoxes of his self-birth style: because it does not lead into a common world, but into one's own and alternative worlds, it simulates a coming into the world in order not to be born. In this way, a paradoxical and monstrous move enters the birth movement. It does lead "out," but it does not lead to anyone; it does bring something "forth," but it withdraws it in the same gesture. In Zarathustra's "Night Song," Nietzsche has provided the formulas for this: "But I live in my own light, I drink back into myself the flames that break out of me. ... A hunger grows out of my beauty; I wish to harm those for whom I shine, I wish to rob those on whom I have bestowed. ... Withdrawing my hand when a hand already reaches for it; hesitating like the waterfall that hesitates even while plunging." Friedrich Nietzsche, *Thus Spoke Zarathustra*, trans. Adrian del Caro, eds. Adrian del Caro and Robert Pippin (Cambridge: Cambridge University Press, 2006), pp. 81–2. The paradoxical phantasms of a birth into verticality, of a standing there "the way one is born," belong to this paradox of overspending without contributing. Through these paradoxical gestures and as soon as it begins with its own bringing forth, the subject becomes a mother who does not place real children into the world but monsters of self-reliance, motherless self-standers,

works, doctrines, law tables, erected things of any kind, that which has been thrown out and thrown down.

15 [The two definitive English translations of Heidegger's *Sein und Zeit* are *Being and Time*, trans. Joan Stambaugh, rev. Dennis J. Schmidt (Albany: State University of New York Press, 2010) and *Being and Time*, trans. John Macquarrie and Edward Robinson (Oxford: Blackwell Publishers, 1962).]

16 ["Enframing" is a standard translation for Heidegger's concept of *"Gestell,"* which he defines as the essence of modern technology. *"Gestell"* can also be thought of as rack, structure, frame, or skeleton. "Enframing" is the way that being reveals itself to humans by challenging us to see all things as a standing reserve waiting to be used up. See Martin Heidegger, *The Question Concerning Technology and Other Essays*, trans. Martin Lovitt (New York: Grandland Publishing Inc., 1977).]

17 [An allusion to Nietzsche, *Thus Spoke Zarathustra*, p. 117: "Thoughts that come on the feet of doves steer the world."]

18 Lloyd deMause presents a bold attempt in this direction – certainly away from the ontological problem – in *Foundations of Psychohistory* (New York: Creative Roots, 1982), Chapter 7: "The Fetal Origins of History."

19 Hans Saner rightly pointed out the traces of an awareness that being exists "birthingly" in Heidegger's *Being and Time*. But it was only Thomas H. Macho who has recently shown a latent natality thinking in Heidegger by way of an ingenious interpretation: "Being-there means: having been placed into nothingness. An attempt to understand Heidegger's talks on death ..." (Lecture for the Philosophical Society Graz, 1987).

20 In *Lebenszeit und Weltzeit*, Hans Blumenberg reveals (among other things) the extent to which this will to not having been extends – the position of an unconsciousness at birth is affirmed with phenomenological authority: "Every human finds out that they were born by being told, since they were not there to experience it." *Lebenszeit und Weltzeit* (Frankfurt: Suhrkamp, 1986), p. 91.

21 [Lao Tsu, *Tao Te Ching*, trans. Gia-Fu Feng and Jane English (London: Wildwood House, 1991), p. 11.]

Chapter 4 The Fundamental and the Urgent – or: The Tao of Politics

1 [English: "It's hard not to write satire." See: Juvenal, *The Satires*, trans. Niall Rudd (Oxford: Oxford University Press, 1991), p. 4.]

2 [Johannes Rau (1931–2006) was a politician in Germany's Social Democratic Party (SPD).]

3 [Klaus Staeck (b. 1931) is a German lawyer and publisher. He is best known for his graphic work, which includes satirical political posters. Paul Lorenzen (1915–94) was a German philosopher and mathematician. He was one of the founders of the Erlangen School and co-inventor of game semantics.]

4 The ontological motives are not discussed here; they have been

interpreted in the previous chapter as self-birthing efforts of a subjectivity that builds its own worlds.

5 [This refers to the Intermediate-Range Nuclear Forces (INF) Treaty
   signed by Reagan and Gorbachev, which eliminated a class of nuclear
   weapons and restricted the deployment of missiles.]
6 [Kafka, *A Hunger Artist and Other Stories*, p. 193.]
7 [Friedrich Hölderlin, "Patmos," in *Hyperion and Other Poems*, trans.
   Michael Hamburger (New York: Continuum Publishing Company,
   2002), p. 245.]

Chapter 5 Paris Aphorisms on Rationality

Originally written for a Franco-German philosophy colloquium in
February 1986 at the Pompidou Centre in Paris.

1 [Jean Maurel, *Victor Hugo, philosophe* (Paris: Presses Universitaires de
   France, 1985), p. 10: "Philosophers, one more effort if you want to be
   Parisians!"]
2 [Bertolt Brecht. In "Philosophizing Brecht: An (In)conclusion," trans.
   Norman Roessler, in Norman Roessler and Anthony Squiers (eds.),
   *Philosophizing Brecht: Critical Readings on Art, Consciousness, Social
   Theory and Performance* (Leiden: Konilke Brill NV, 2019), pp. 180–1.]
3 [See René Descartes, *Discourse on Method*, trans. Richard Kennington
   (Indianapolis: Hackett, 2007), p. 15: "Good sense is the best distributed
   thing in the world." The author uses the original French for the title of
   this section.]
4 [See chapter 2, pp. 44–5]
5 [A line from René Char's poem "Les Dentelles de Montmirail" (1960).]

Chapter 6 After Modernity

1 [Samuel Beckett, *Endgame* (New York: Grove Press, 1957), p. 20.]
2 Cf. Arnold Gehlen, *Zeit-Bilder*, 3rd edn (Frankfurt: Vittorio
   Klostermann Verlag,1986), pp. 202f. Keyword "Repristination."
3 Cf. Günther Anders, *Endzeit und Zeitende: Gedankern über die atomare
   Situation* (Munich: Beck, 1979).
4 With Paul, both still coincide with one another.
5 To this we can add a speculation about the "end of history": if the
   content of the Christian world history were indeed the universal
   dissemination of a message, it would end in the moment where the
   assumption of a significant time-frame for the spread of this message
   was no longer necessary. Thus, history in the traditional sense would
   be determined by the slowness of the message. From a certain speed of
   message-transmission on, the effect of history disintegrates. *Apostolic
   historicism* gets replaced by a *planetary information technology*. History
   is the time of media installations – post-history, the era of the program.
   If historical politics becomes installation politics, then post-historical
   politics turns to program politics.
6 At the same time, this means that there is nothing more ironic and

melancholy than the conflict between religion and state in the so-called "socialist" countries.

7 [Bloch, *Experimentum Mundi*, p. 228.]
8 See, for example, Lloyd deMause, *Reagan's America.* (New York: Creative Roots Inc. Publishers, 1984).
9 Cf. Falk Wagner, *Geld oder Gott? Zur Geldbestimmtheit der kulturellen und religiösen Lebenswelt* (Stuttgart: Klett-Cotta, 1985).
10 [Franz Kafka. *The Blue Octavo Notebooks*, trans. Ernst Kaiser and Eithne Wilkins (Cambridge, Mass.: Exact Change, 1991), p. 22.]
11 Kah Kyung Cho brilliantly explores these questions in a book that the author regrets not having known prior to his own attempts: *Bewußtsein und Natursein: Phänomenologischer West-Ost-Diwan* (Freiburg/Munich: K. Alber, 1987).
12 [See chapter 3, n. 16.]
13 [E.M. Cioran, *The Trouble with Being Born*, trans. Richard Howard (New York: Arcade Publishing, 2011), p. 204.]
14 [See Walter Benjamin. "Theses on the Philosophy of History," *Illuminations*, trans. Harry Zohn (New York: Schocken Books, 1969), p. 249.]
15 [Bloch, *Experimentum Mundi*, p. 230.]